# LECTURE READY 1

## SECOND EDITION

STRATEGIES FOR
Academic Listening
and Speaking

W9-BQY-975

PEG SAROSY
KATHY SHERAK

OXFORD
UNIVERSITY PRESS

# OXFORD
## UNIVERSITY PRESS

198 Madison Avenue
New York, NY 10016 USA

Great Clarendon Street, Oxford, OX2 6DP, United Kingdom

Oxford University Press is a department of the University of Oxford.
It furthers the University's objective of excellence in research, scholarship,
and education by publishing worldwide. Oxford is a registered trade
mark of Oxford University Press in the UK and in certain other countries

© Oxford University Press 2013

The moral rights of the author have been asserted

First published in 2013

2017 2016 2015

10 9 8 7 6 5

**No unauthorized photocopying**

All rights reserved. No part of this publication may be reproduced,
stored in a retrieval system, or transmitted, in any form or by any means, without
the prior permission in writing of Oxford University Press,
or as expressly permitted by law, by licence or under terms agreed with the
appropriate reprographics rights organization. Enquiries concerning reproduction
outside the scope of the above should be sent to the
ELT Rights Department, Oxford University Press, at the address above

You must not circulate this work in any other form and you must impose this same
condition on any acquirer

Links to third party websites are provided by Oxford in good faith and for
information only. Oxford disclaims any responsibility for the materials contained
in any third party website referenced in this work

General Manager, American ELT: Laura Pearson
Publisher: Stephanie Karras
Associate Publishing Manager: Sharon Sargent
Development Editor: Rebecca Mostov
Director, ADP: Susan Sanguily
Executive Design Manager: Maj-Britt Hagsted
Electronic Production Manager: Julie Armstrong
Designer: Debbie Lofaso
Production Artists: Julie Sussman-Perez, Elissa Santos
Image Manager: Trisha Masterson
Image Editor: Liaht Pashayan
Production Coordinator: Christopher Espejo

ISBN: 978 0 19 441727 3    LECTURE READY 1

Printed in China

This book is printed on paper from certified and well-managed sources

ACKNOWLEDGEMENTS

*Illustrations by*: Arthur Mount, p93.

*We would also like to thank the following for permission to reproduce the following
photographs*: Cover, Jan Greune/Getty Images, AP Photo/Franka Bruns; vi (cover
reduction photo) MARTIN RUETSCHI/Keystone/Corbis; vii Purestock/Getty Images;
ix Marcin Krygier/istockphoto.com; xi Ismail Akin Bostanci/istockphoto.com; p1
Purestock/Getty Images; p2 (bottom) Radius Images/Alamy, (top) imagebroker.net/
SuperStock; p10 Erik Isakson/Getty Images; p11 OUP/Purestock; p23 David Parker/
Alamy; p25 Image Source/Alamy; p27 Zero Creatives/Getty Images; p28 (car)
Jim West/Alamy, (phone) hanibaram/istockphoto.com, (GPS) kaczor58/
shutterstock.com; p36 Troy House/Corbis; p37 kristian sekulic/istockphoto.com;
p39 OUP/Corbis/Digital Stock; p40 Linda Steward/istockphoto.com; p44 rubberball/
Getty Images; p48 Purestock/SuperStock/Corbis; p49 OUP/Digital Vision; p51
Fotosearch Premium/Getty Images; p53 Horst Herget/Masterfile; p54 Andrew
Hobbs/Getty Images; p62 Echo/Getty Images; p65 OUP/Hill Street Studios;
p66 (computer) Edward Mallia/istockphoto.com, (mp3) Anthony Brown/
istockphoto.com, (files) OUP/image100, (etchings) Hadrian/shutterstock.com;
p74 René Mansi/istockphoto.com; p75 Purestock/Getty Images; p76 Celia Peterson/
arabianEye/Corbis; p79 Leontura/Getty Images; p88 Mark Hatfield/istockphoto.
com; p89 OUP/RubberBall; p92 (beach) OUP/Dinodia Images, (river, mountains)
OUP/Photodisc, (desert) OUP/Mark Phillips; p98 Ocean/Corbis; p100
OUP/Photodisc; p105 Rob Melnychuk/Getty Images; p106 (1,3)
Blue Lantern Studio/Corbis, (2) Hulton Archive/Getty Images,
(4) Lebrecht Authors/Lebrecht Music & Arts/Corbis; p107 Stefano
Bianchetti/Corbis; p112 Fuse/Getty Images; p118 (1) OUP/Images
& Stories, (2) OUP/Image Source, (3) Kenneth Johansson/Corbis,
(4) OUP/Photographers Choice; p119 (London) Jason Hawkes/Corbis,
(Sydney) OUP/Photodisc; p124 Vespasian/Alamy; p126 STOCK4B-RF/
Getty Images; p127 Momatiuk - Eastcott/Corbis.

# ACKNOWLEDGEMENTS

**We would like to acknowledge the following individuals for their input during the development of the series:**

**ELLEN BARRETT**
Wayne State University
Michigan, U.S.A.

**DAVID BUNK**
Portland State University
Oregon, U.S.A.

**SAMANTHA BURNS**
Dhofar University
Oman

**SHIOW-WEN CHEN**
Cheng Hsiu University
Kaohsiung

**ELAINE COCKERHAM**
Higher College of Technology
Oman

**HITOSHI EGUCHI**
Hokusei Gakuen University
Sapporo, Japan

**TRACY FALCONER**
University of Nebraska at Kearney
Nebraska, U.S.A.

**JONATHAN FREEDMAN**
Srinakharinwirot University
Bangkok, Thailand

**JAMES HARMAN**
Kanto Kokusai Koto Gakko
Tokyo, Japan

**HASSAN HAWASH**
Abu Dhabi Men's College
The United Arab Emirates

**MARGARET LAYTON**
University of Nevada
Nevada, U.S.A.

**WILLIAM LITTLE**
Georgetown University
Washington DC, U.S.A.

**JESSICA MATCHETT**
Handong Global University
Pohang, South Korea

**FERNANDA ORTIZ**
CESL, University of Arizona
Arizona, U.S.A.

**GABOR PINTER**
Kobe University
Kobe, Japan

**JOHN RACINE**
Dokkyo University
Saitama, Japan

**STEPHANIE STEWART**
University of Houston
Texas, U.S.A.

**WARUNWAN TANGSUWAN**
Slipakorn University
Bangkok, Thailand

**JAKCHAI YIMNGAM**
Rajamangala University of Technology
Phra Nakhon
Bangkok, Thailand

# LECTURE READY 1
# CONTENTS

## STUDENT BOOKS

## iTOOLS FOR ALL LEVELS

**GO ONLINE DIGITAL DOWNLOAD CENTER**

## Lecture Ready

- Prepares students for listening, note taking, and academic discussion through videos of realistic and engaging lectures.

- Explicit presentation skills prepare students for public speaking, a requirement in today's academic and professional world.

- Audio and video available through the Lecture Ready Digital Download Center, www.lectureready.com/student, allows students to study anytime, anywhere.

- Video-based assessment tracks progress to show what students have mastered and where they still need help.

*Lecture Ready: Strategies for Academic Listening and Speaking* **guides students through the complete academic process.**

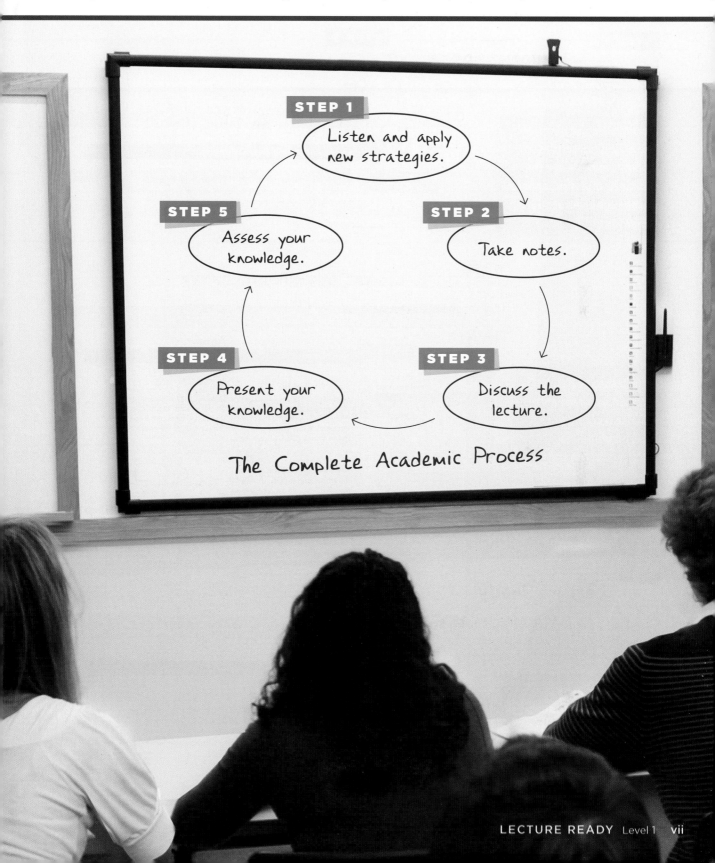

STEP 1
Listen and apply new strategies.

STEP 2
Take notes.

STEP 3
Discuss the lecture.

STEP 4
Present your knowledge.

STEP 5
Assess your knowledge.

The Complete Academic Process

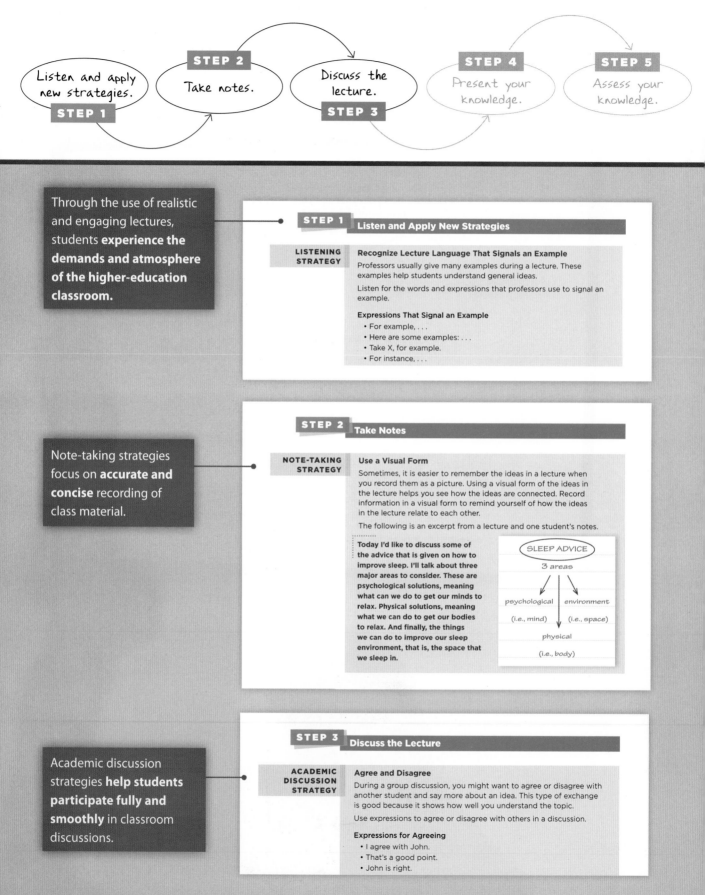

**STEP 1** — Listen and apply new strategies.

**STEP 2** — Take notes.

**STEP 3** — Discuss the lecture.

**STEP 4** — Present your knowledge.

**STEP 5** — Assess your knowledge.

Through the use of realistic and engaging lectures, students **experience the demands and atmosphere of the higher-education classroom.**

### STEP 1 — Listen and Apply New Strategies

**LISTENING STRATEGY**

**Recognize Lecture Language That Signals an Example**

Professors usually give many examples during a lecture. These examples help students understand general ideas.

Listen for the words and expressions that professors use to signal an example.

**Expressions That Signal an Example**
- For example, . . .
- Here are some examples: . . .
- Take X, for example.
- For instance, . . .

Note-taking strategies focus on **accurate and concise** recording of class material.

### STEP 2 — Take Notes

**NOTE-TAKING STRATEGY**

**Use a Visual Form**

Sometimes, it is easier to remember the ideas in a lecture when you record them as a picture. Using a visual form of the ideas in the lecture helps you see how the ideas are connected. Record information in a visual form to remind yourself of how the ideas in the lecture relate to each other.

The following is an excerpt from a lecture and one student's notes.

**Today I'd like to discuss some of the advice that is given on how to improve sleep. I'll talk about three major areas to consider. These are psychological solutions, meaning what can we do to get our minds to relax. Physical solutions, meaning what we can do to get our bodies to relax. And finally, the things we can do to improve our sleep environment, that is, the space that we sleep in.**

> SLEEP ADVICE
> 3 areas
> psychological (i.e., mind)    environment (i.e., space)
> physical (i.e., body)

Academic discussion strategies **help students participate fully and smoothly** in classroom discussions.

### STEP 3 — Discuss the Lecture

**ACADEMIC DISCUSSION STRATEGY**

**Agree and Disagree**

During a group discussion, you might want to agree or disagree with another student and say more about an idea. This type of exchange is good because it shows how well you understand the topic.

Use expressions to agree or disagree with others in a discussion.

**Expressions for Agreeing**
- I agree with John.
- That's a good point.
- John is right.

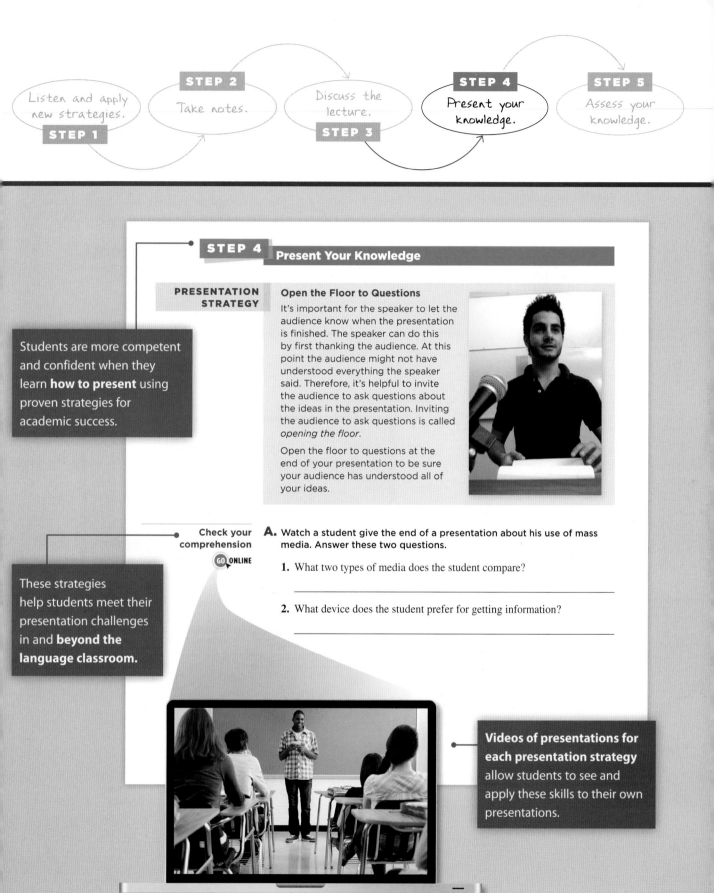

## STEP 1
Listen and apply new strategies.

## STEP 2
Take notes.

## STEP 3
Discuss the lecture.

## STEP 4
Present your knowledge.

## STEP 5
Assess your knowledge.

---

### STEP 4 — Present Your Knowledge

**PRESENTATION STRATEGY**

**Open the Floor to Questions**

It's important for the speaker to let the audience know when the presentation is finished. The speaker can do this by first thanking the audience. At this point the audience might not have understood everything the speaker said. Therefore, it's helpful to invite the audience to ask questions about the ideas in the presentation. Inviting the audience to ask questions is called *opening the floor*.

Open the floor to questions at the end of your presentation to be sure your audience has understood all of your ideas.

Students are more competent and confident when they learn **how to present** using proven strategies for academic success.

These strategies help students meet their presentation challenges in and **beyond the language classroom.**

**Check your comprehension**

**GO ONLINE**

**A.** Watch a student give the end of a presentation about his use of mass media. Answer these two questions.

**1.** What two types of media does the student compare?

_____

**2.** What device does the student prefer for getting information?

_____

**Videos of presentations for each presentation strategy** allow students to see and apply these skills to their own presentations.

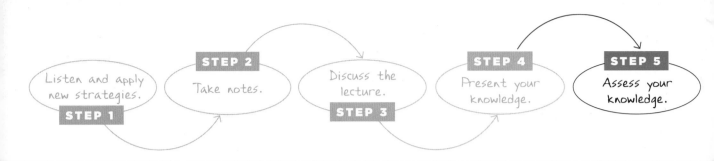

| STEP 1 | STEP 2 | STEP 3 | STEP 4 | STEP 5 |
|---|---|---|---|---|
| Listen and apply new strategies. | Take notes. | Discuss the lecture. | Present your knowledge. | Assess your knowledge. |

# Video-based tests track progress to show what students have mastered and where they still need help.

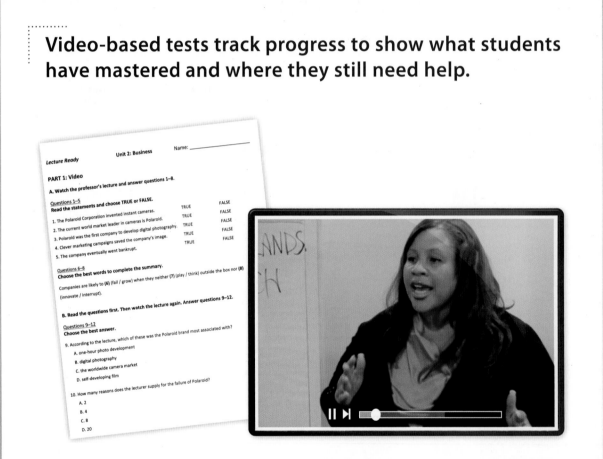

**GO ONLINE** **Lecture Ready Assessment Program**

Unit, midterm, and final exams can be found on iTools or www.lectureready.com/teacher.

- **CUSTOMIZABLE** Adapt tests to meet the precise needs of students.

- **EFFECTIVE** Prepare student for standardized tests.

- **ENGAGING** All tests are based on **100% NEW video content**.

# Lecture Ready Student Resources

## CONNECT

Downloadable video and audio allow students to study **anytime, anywhere**.

## ENGAGE

Students fully engage in the learning experience by **downloading and watching** each chapter's lecture and student presentation models.

## ASSESS

Video-based unit, midterm, and final exams allow on-going assesment.

---

Lecture Ready | Unit 2: Business | Name: _____

**PART 1: Video**

**A. Watch the professor's lecture and answer questions 1–8.**

Questions 1–5
Read the statements and choose TRUE or FALSE.

| | | |
|---|---|---|
| 1. The Polaroid Corporation invented instant cameras. | TRUE | FALSE |
| 2. The current world market leader in cameras is Polaroid. | TRUE | FALSE |
| 3. Polaroid was the first company to develop digital photography. | TRUE | FALSE |
| 4. Clever marketing campaigns saved the company's image. | TRUE | FALSE |
| 5. The company eventually went bankrupt. | TRUE | FALSE |

Questions 6–8
Choose the best words to complete the summary.

Companies are likely to **(6)** (fail / grow) when they neither **(7)** (play / think) outside the box nor **(8)** (innovate / interrupt).

**B. Read the questions first. Then watch the lecture again. Answer questions 9–12.**

Questions 9–12
Choose the best answer.

9. According to the lecture, which of these was the Polaroid brand most associated with?

   A. one-hour photo development

   B. digital photography

   C. the worldwide camera market

   D. self-developing film

---

**IT'S EASY! Use the access code printed on the inside back cover of this book to download video and audio at** <u>www.lectureready.com/student</u>.

*Lecture Ready iTools* bring the book, video, and audio together in one classroom presentation tool.

- For use with an LCD projector or interactive whiteboard
- Full student book for in-class viewing
- All video and audio links at point of use for whole-class presentations
- Unit, midterm, and final tests based on 100% NEW additional video content available as click-and-print PDFs and customizable Word documents
- Answer Keys and Teaching Notes

## Teacher Digital Download Center

Go to www.lectureready.com/teacher. See your local representative to order a Teacher Resource Access Code.

For additional support email our customer support team at eltsupport@oup.com.

# Unit Goals

# Psychology

psychology \saɪˈkɑlədʒi\ The study of the mind and the way that people behave

## CHAPTER 1

**Learn about the expectations of college professors**

### Listening Strategies

- Build background knowledge to understand lectures
- Recognize types of information in lectures
- Use background knowledge to predict content in lectures

### Note-Taking Strategies

- Leave out the least important words in a lecture
- Assess and revise your notes after a lecture

### Academic Discussion Strategy

- Show interest during the academic discussion

### Presentation Strategy

- Use eye contact and good posture to show authority and confidence

## CHAPTER 2

**Learn about the pace of life in different places**

### Listening Strategy

- Recognize lecture language

### Note-Taking Strategies

- Write down the words with the most meaning in a lecture
- After lectures, summarize what you heard

### Academic Discussion Strategy

- Lead the group discussion

### Presentation Strategy

- Use hand gestures to show authority and confidence

**LISTENING STRATEGY**

**Build Background Knowledge to Understand Lectures**

Before you go to a lecture, think about what you already know about the lecture's topic. Complete any reading assignments. Then discuss your reading with classmates. This will give you necessary background information and vocabulary that will prepare you for the lecture.

**Think about the topic**

**A.** Look at the pictures. Think about what the professor and students are doing in each photo. Then work with a partner to answer the questions below.

- How are the photos different?
- What are the goals of the students in each photo?
- How are these classes similar to or different from classes you've been in?

**Read to build background knowledge**
See page 2

**B.** Read this page from a professor's Web site. It contains information for students enrolled in her course.

# Syllabus
## *Psychology 210: Introduction to Social Psychology*

### OBJECTIVES
Social psychology is the study of the way people think, feel, and behave in social situations. The purpose of this course is to:
- teach students the basic principles of social psychology
- show the importance of social psychology
- prepare students for further study in social psychology

### GENERAL INFORMATION
| | |
|---|---|
| Instructor's Name: | Dr. Jennifer Lindley |
| Office Phone and Email: | PH (373) 555-1233, jlindley@unop.edu |
| Office Hours: | MW 1:00–2:00, other times by appointment |

### TEXTBOOKS
*Time Across Cultures,* by Dr. Gabriel Chan
*Social Life: Studies in Social Psychology,* by Dr. Maggie Baird

### REQUIREMENTS AND ASSIGNMENTS
4 exams on **lectures** and reading **assignments**: 2 quizzes, 1 midterm exam, 1 final exam
1 class presentation
2 one-page opinion papers
Attendance (This includes how much you **participate** in **class discussions**.)

### GRADING POLICY
Course **Components**
| | |
|---|---|
| Quizzes | 20% |
| Midterm exam | 20% |
| Final exam | 25% |
| Papers and presentation | 20% |
| Attendance | 15% |

### EXPECTATIONS
- Attend class regularly.
- Do the reading assignments before class.
- Turn in assignments when they are due (on or before due date).
- Do your own work.
- Participate in discussions: Share your ideas, and listen to other students' ideas.
- Contact me if you have any problems or questions.

**C.** Answer these questions about the reading. Then discuss your answers
with a partner.

1. What will the students learn in this course?

*In This cours they are going to learn about psycholgy.*

2. What is the grading policy for this course?

*Quizzes, Participate in Class discussion, A Attendece final excim.*

3. What does attendance include?

*Atted class cegulary.*

**D.** Match the words from the reading with their definitions. Look back at
the reading on page 3 to check your answers.

| | | |
|---|---|---|
| _c_ **1.** syllabus | **a.** | what you think or hope will happen |
| _d_ **2.** objective | **b.** | one of the parts that together form something |
| _e_ **3.** lecture | **c.** | a professor's plan for a course |
| _f_ **4.** assignment | **d.** | a goal or purpose |
| _g_ **5.** participate | **e.** | a long talk given to a group of people, usually students |
| _h_ **6.** class discussion | **f.** | a piece of work that a professor requires his or her students to do |
| **7.** component | **g.** | to share or join in an activity |
| expectation | **h.** | the students of a class talking about a topic related to their classwork |

e phrase with a similar meaning to the underlined idiom.

nts didn't understand why the professor assigned the article.
rofessor used information from the article in her lecture.
idents get the picture.

sed    **b.** understand clearly    **c.** look at photographs

**Discuss the reading**   **F.** Discuss these questions in a group. Share your answers with the class.

  **1.** If you were a student in Professor Lindley's class, which of her expectations would be new and maybe difficult for you?

  **2.** In her syllabus, Professor Lindley writes in two places that students must participate in discussions. Why do you think she has listed this twice?

**Review what you know**   **G.** With a partner, discuss three things that you have learned from the reading and from your discussion about the professor's syllabus.

  **1.** _____

  _____

  **2.** _____

  _____

  **3.** _____

  _____

**Prepare for the listening strategy**   **H.** To help you understand the listening strategy, discuss the situation below with a partner. Then answer the question.

A friend of yours is getting ready to go to his first university lecture. He says to you, "I read the textbook. What type of information will be in the professor's lecture that I haven't already learned from the textbook?"

What would you tell your friend?

**LISTENING STRATEGY**

**Recognize Types of Information Included in Lectures**

A lecture is a long talk by a professor about a particular topic. During a lecture, a professor often gives more information about a topic students have read about in their textbook. Often the professor will also explain details about the topic to help students better understand what they've read.

**Types of Information Professors Include in Lectures**
- examples
- facts and data
- history
- background information
- survey results
- theories
- research study

**I.** Read these excerpts from three different social psychology lectures on three different topics. Match each excerpt to one of these types of information:

**a.** research study     **b.** facts and data     **c.** history

_C_ **1.** OK. Let me move on. We're going into more details about this course. Before I move on, I want to say that it's important to know how the field of social psychology developed. We began to see many articles written about social psychology around the end of the 19th century. Then, around 1903–1908, the field of social psychology was introduced. But in the mid-1920s, social psychology really became its own subject.

_a_ **2.** Hi, everyone. Good morning. Today I will be talking about how what we smell influences our emotions. I want to tell you about some interesting research done in Germany in 2007. Researchers found that they could use certain smells to create memories in the brains of people while they were sleeping. The scientists reported that the people could remember their memories better because of the smell.

_b_ **3.** All right. Now, there are many ways that people behave during a bad economy. Let's look at some interesting numbers: One thing we learned is that one in ten—that's 10 percent—of U.S. workers have increased the amount of snacking—I mean eating junk food—during the day. Also, 43 percent have gained weight in their current job. So let's talk about what these statistics mean.

**J.** Study the meaning of these general academic words. Fill in the blanks with the correct words in the correct form. Compare your answers with a partner.

> **point out:** to make people notice something, usually by telling them
>
> **theory:** an idea that is used to explain something

The professor _____ that many people have never studied social psychology.

This means that the _____ about how people behave will be new to students.

**NOTE-TAKING STRATEGY**

**Leave Out Words That Are Not Very Meaningful**

While listening to lectures, students may try to write down every word the professor says. However, it is almost impossible to keep up with the lecture using this method. Instead, students should write down only the most important ideas.

When you take notes, leave out words that are not meaningful. Write down only the most important information.

Read this excerpt from a lecture on social psychology. Then look at one student's notes from the lecture.

**Social psychology is the study of the way people behave and how people feel about social situations. So we will learn about what people think about other people and how they think about society . . . and how they behave together.**

Social psychology

Study – way people behave, how people feel

– social situations

We: learn what people think about other people, how they

think about society, behave together

The words that are not important to the meaning of the professor's ideas are usually in these categories:

**pronouns:** *our, my, their* . . .  **prepositions:** *in, on, at* . . .

**helping verbs:** *be, have, do* . . .  **conjunctions:** *and, but, so* . . .

**determiners:** *a, the, this* . . .

---

**Leave out words that are not meaningful**

**A.** Look at the sample excerpt and notes above. In the excerpt, cross out words that are not in the notes.

**B.** Read these sentences from a lecture on social psychology. Take notes. Leave out any words that are not important to the professor's ideas.

**1.** In this class, you will participate in discussions and listen to lectures.

_____

**2.** I will show you the importance of social psychology.

_____

**Predict the Lecture's Content from Your Background Knowledge**

To help you get ready to learn new information and listen more actively, think about what the professor might discuss in the lecture. Think about everything you already know about the topic, and make a prediction about what the professor will discuss.

Make predictions

**C.** Before the lecture, think about everything you have learned and discussed about Professor Lindley's syllabus for the social psychology class. What do you expect to learn from the lecture? Write three predictions below. Compare your predictions with a partner.

1.  I expect to learn more about *to help People.*   *People.*
2.  *I expect to learn more about to understand*
3.  *I expect to learn the People Feel.*

Watch the lecture

GO ONLINE

**D.** Watch the lecture, and take notes. Remember to leave out words that are not very meaningful.

*online (توضيح)*
*معلومات عن*

Topic: *social Psychology 210*

General information about social psychology:

*How people interested with other People*

*الشرح عن الـ lecture*

Objective: *Help become more interestd in the Field Psychology.*

*معلومات عن*

Information about the readings, lectures, and discussions:

*get the assignment do reading, lectures informatid disussson also questen dissussion*

*معلومات عن الدرجة*

Information about the grade:

*Quizzes and exam and notes and opinion Paper*

*الحضور*

Attendance:

*You need To PArticiPate in Class decussion.*

**E.** Check the statement that best describes how well you were able to
understand the lecture.

_____ I was able to understand all the ideas in the lecture.

_____ I was able to understand most of the ideas in the lecture.

_____ I was able to understand only a few of the ideas in the lecture.

**F.** Use your notes to answer these questions.

1. What will the students study in this course?

socail psychology
_____

_____

2. What will the professor do in the lectures?

_____

_____

_____

3. What does the professor want the students to do during the discussions?

_____

_____

4. What are the two parts of attendance?

_____

_____

**Assess and Revise Your Notes**

During a lecture, you might miss an important piece of information
that the professor gives, such as a word, definition, or idea. To check
that your notes are complete, compare your notes with classmates in
a study group after the lecture. Add any information that you missed
in your notes.

**G.** Were you able to answer the questions in Exercise F using the
information in your notes? Compare and discuss your notes with a
few other students. Help each other fill in any missing information.
Revise your notes.

**ACADEMIC DISCUSSION STRATEGY**

### Show Interest During the Discussion

Your professors will often ask you to discuss the ideas in a lecture with a group of students in the classroom. During these discussions, professors expect students to participate actively. Active participation includes paying attention and letting the person who is speaking know that you are interested. Use actions and expressions to show that you are interested and paying attention when other students speak during the discussion.

### Actions That People Use to Show Interest During the Group Discussion
- Make eye contact with the speaker.
- Nod your head when something is important or when you want to show that you understand or agree.
- Write down ideas that you think are interesting or important.

### Expressions for Showing Interest During the Group Discussion
- Uh-huh.
- Hmm.
- That's interesting.
- Wow!
- I get it.
- I see.

**List more examples**

**A.** Work with a partner to think of other actions and expressions for showing interest during a group discussion. Write your examples here.

_____

_____

_____

**B.** In a group, read and discuss the questions. Keep the conversation going until every student has had a chance to practice showing interest during a discussion.

1. Do you prefer taking courses that have 75 or more students in them, or do you prefer courses with fewer students? Why?

2. Is it better to sit in the front of the classroom during a lecture or in the back? Why?

**C.** Discuss these ideas with your classmates. Remember to use expressions, words, and phrases that show interest.

1. The professor says that some class time will be used for discussions. How do you feel about spending time in class discussing ideas with the professor and with classmates?

2. Why do you think professors want students to contribute their own ideas and opinions?

3. Imagine you were a student in the class you saw in the lecture. What would be difficult for you? What would be easy for you? If I was

4. Look back at your notes. What was another idea in the lecture that you found important or interesting? Tell the class why you think it is important or interesting. Ask for your classmates' opinions.

**PRESENTATION STRATEGY**

### Use Good Posture and Eye Contact

Both a speaker's words and a speaker's body language communicate with the audience. Two important aspects of body language are posture and eye contact. A speaker's good posture—the way a person sits, stands, or walks—tells the audience that the speaker is confident. Looking directly into the eyes of people in the audience helps the audience stay interested. As a result, they follow the speaker's ideas.

Use good posture and eye contact to keep your audience interested and to show confidence.

**Check your comprehension**

GO ONLINE

**A.** Watch a student give a presentation in which he introduces himself to his Social Psychology class. Answer these two questions.

1. Where is the student from?

_____

2. What is one thing that is going to be difficult for him?

_____

**Notice posture and eye contact**

GO ONLINE

**B.** Watch the video again. Think about the information in the strategy box above. In your notebook, list two problems with the student's posture and eye contact.

GO ONLINE **C.** The student received some suggestions about the presentation and delivered it again. Watch the new presentation. In your notebook, list two improvements the student made to his posture. Then list two improvements he made to his eye contact to better show confidence and keep the audience interested.

**PRESENTATION STRATEGY**

### Strategies for Using Good Posture
- Stand up straight, and don't slouch.
- Hold your head high.
- Avoid moving back and forth.

**List more examples**

**D.** Work with a partner to think of other examples of good posture that shows confidence. Write your examples in your notebook.

**Strategies for Using Good Eye Contact**
- Look at the entire audience, not just a few people.
- Move your head around so you can make eye contact with people in all parts of the room.
- Avoid looking at the floor or out a window.

**List more examples**

**E.** Work with a partner to think of other ways to make eye contact that shows confidence and keeps the audience interested. Write your examples here.

_____

_____

_____

**Practice good posture and eye contact**

**F.** Stand in front of a group of classmates. Tell them your name, your favorite color, and your favorite animal. Explain why you like the color and animal.

After you finish, have your classmates give you feedback on your eye contact and posture. Ask them these two questions:

**1.** What are two things I did well with my posture and eye contact?

**2.** What is one way to improve my posture and eye contact?

**Give a presentation**

**G.** Develop and deliver a presentation about yourself.

Introduce yourself, and share one thing about this class that will be a challenge and one thing that you are excited about. Then tell your audience what you want to study in the future.

Use the strategies for good posture and eye contact to show confidence and keep the audience interested.

Before you prepare your presentation, review the ideas and vocabulary from this chapter.

# CHAPTER 2 The Pace of a Place

**STEP 1** | **Listen and Apply New Strategies**

**Think about the topic**

**A.** Answer the questions in the survey to find out about your personal pace of life.

## What Is Your Relationship with Time?

**What best describes you? For each question, answer yes or no.**

| | Yes | No |
|---|---|---|
| **1.** Do you frequently look at your watch or a clock? | ✓ | ☐ |
| **2.** Do you always know the time and what day of the week it is? | ☐ | ✓ |
| **3.** Are you often the first person finished eating at the table? | ☐ | ✓ |
| **4.** Do you sometimes skip meals or eat them very quickly? | ✓ | ☐ |
| **5.** Do you walk faster than most people? | ✓ | ☐ |
| **6.** When driving in traffic, do you get annoyed when drivers move slowly? | ✓ | ☐ |
| **7.** Do you get more annoyed than most people if you have to wait in line for more than a couple of minutes at the bank or a store? | ✓ | ☐ |

*If you answered yes to most of the questions above, you tend to live life at a hurried pace.*

*If you answered no to most of the questions above, you tend to live life at a more relaxed pace.*

**1.** Compare your answers with a classmate. Are they similar or different?

**2.** How would you describe your pace of life? Give examples to explain your answer.

**3.** Which is better, a hurried or relaxed pace of life? Why?

**B.** Read this article about each person's unique pace of life.

# The Beat of Your Own Drum

Are you a slow person or a fast person? Do you like to stay busy, or do you enjoy doing nothing sometimes? Do you prefer the highway or country roads?

We all know that the **pace** of life is different in different places and **cultures**. When we visit a place for the first time, we get a general idea of the place and what life is like there. The pace of life helps to form this general impression. The pace of life in a city, for example, is a big part of its unique **atmosphere**.

This isn't just true for cities and countries, however. There are also big differences in pace between individuals, even individuals within the same culture living in the same town. Next-door neighbors can experience life at completely different paces.

Researchers want to get an **accurate** idea about why individuals have different ideas about time and pace of life. To study this, they look at people's ideas of "time urgency." Time urgency is the effort a person makes to **achieve** as much as possible in a given amount of time. Everyone has his or her own **sense** of time urgency. Some people feel the need to try to achieve a lot, while other people have the **tendency** to set their goals lower and achieve less.

When asked about the pace of their lives, people tend to think about several things: the speed they feel at their workplace, the level of activity they prefer in their personal lives, and the level of activity they prefer in the environment around them. To **assess** the pace of your own life, ask yourself these questions:

Do you feel the pace of your life is too fast, too slow, or just right when it comes to:

- school or work life?
- the city or town where you live?
- home life?
- social life?
- life as a whole?

You don't need a psychologist to understand your answers to these questions. The fact is that what is too fast for one person might be boring for another. There is nothing good or bad about an individual's pace of life. Each of us simply **marches to the beat of his or her own drum.**

**C.** With a partner, discuss these questions about the reading.

1. What does *time urgency* mean?

2. What are three locations that people consider when thinking about the pace of their lives?

3. According to the researchers, which is better, a fast or slow pace of life?

*Back
Pag (15)*

**D.** Circle the answer that correctly completes the definition of the underlined word. Look back at the reading on page 15 to check your answers.

1. <u>Culture</u> is the art, beliefs, behavior, and ideas of _____.

   **a.** a society or group of people   **b.** an individual person

2. <u>Pace</u> is the _____ at which something happens.

   **a.** speed                          **b.** location

3. The <u>atmosphere</u> of a place is _____ the place gives you.

   **a.** the amount of air              **b.** the feeling

4. If information is <u>accurate</u>, it is _____.

   **a.** interesting                    **b.** correct

5. To <u>achieve</u> something means that you _____ in doing it as a result of your actions.

   **a.** fail                           **b.** succeed

6. To have your own <u>sense</u> of a situation means that you have your own _____ about it.

   **a.** feeling                        **b.** specific information

7. To have a <u>tendency</u> toward doing something means that you _____ do it.

   **a.** usually                        **b.** always

8. To <u>assess</u> something means that you make a judgment after thinking _____ about it.

   **a.** carelessly                     **b.** carefully

**E.** Circle the phrase with a similar meaning to the underlined idiom.

City planner Steven Santos won an award for his interesting and original ideas. He really <u>marches to the beat of his own drum</u> and doesn't follow traditional practices.

**a.** follows the rules

**b.** works quickly

**c.** does things in his own way

Discuss the reading **F.** Discuss these questions in a group. Share your answers with the class.

**1.** What are some of the advantages and disadvantages of living life with an extreme sense of time urgency?

**2.** Think about just one or two areas of life mentioned in the article (school, work, city, home, social life), and answer this question:

Do you feel that the pace of your own life is too fast, too slow, or just right? Explain.

Review what you know **G.** With a partner, discuss three things that you have learned from the reading and from your discussion about the pace of life.

**1.** _____

_____

**2.** _____

_____

**3.** _____

_____

Prepare for the listening strategy **H.** To help you understand the listening strategy, discuss the situation below with a partner. Then answer the question.

A friend of yours asks you, "What makes listening to a lecture more difficult than listening to a friend?"

What would you tell your friend?

_____

_____

_____

**Recognize Lecture Language**

Professors know that listening to lectures is challenging for students. They want students to learn, so they try to help students understand the ideas in the lecture. When lecturing, professors use specific words and expressions called *lecture language* to signal:

- what the lecture is about.
- when a new idea is introduced.
- when the meaning of a word is given.
- which information is most important.
- when an example or explanation is introduced.

Listen for the words and expressions that professors use to help you understand a lecture.

---

**Recognize lecture language**

**I.** **Read this excerpt from a lecture about pace and time. Then answer the questions below.**

> Let's look more at the idea of pace and time. To learn about this, researchers asked people about time urgency. So let me define that term: *Time urgency* is the effort a person makes to do as much as possible in a specific amount of time. Does everyone understand that? So when people are asked to measure the time urgency of their own lives, they talk about many things. For instance, they talk about their workplace, they talk about the amount of activity they do, and they also talk about the amount of activity they like to have around them. Let's move on to talk about the ways people measure the pace of their lives at work, around them, and in their daily lives.

What lecture language does the professor use to signal:

**a.** when he or she is giving an example or explanation?

> For instance (define that term)

**b.** when he or she is giving the meaning of a word?

> So let me define that term

**c.** when he or she is moving from one idea to another?

> let's move on

**d.** when he or she is introducing the topic?

> let's look more at the idea

**NOTE-TAKING STRATEGY**

### Write Down the Words with the Most Meaning

You learned that when you take notes, you should omit the professor's words that are not very meaningful. What words should you write in your notes? You should write down the words that have the most meaning in the lecture. In this way, your notes will be useful to you when you study them later.

The words that are important to the meaning of the professor's ideas are usually in these categories:

**nouns:** people, places, things, ideas

**verbs:** actions such as *go, work, walk, sleep, drink*

**adjectives:** description words such as *happy, important, difficult*

**adverbs:** words that describe verbs and often end in *-ly*

---

Write down words with the most meaning

**A.** Read this excerpt from a lecture on the pace of life. Then look at one student's notes from the lecture. Underline the words in the lecture that are in the notes. The first sentence has been done for you.

> The <u>pace of life</u> in the <u>Czech Republic</u> has become <u>more intense since</u> the <u>government changed</u> in <u>1989</u>. One reason for this is that before 1989, people were guaranteed a job. This guarantee of a job resulted in some people working and living at a more leisurely pace.

*Verb* (circled: guaranteed)  *noun* (circled: guarantee)

main Idea:

Pace of life—Czech Republic

gov't

• more intense since government changed—1989 reason:

• before 1989 people guaranteed jobs

• resulted in some people worked/lived more leisurely pace

or bullets / EX.—

**B.** Read this excerpt from another lecture on pace of life. Take notes in your notebook. Write down only the words that have the most meaning.

> Today we'll look at how vacation time . . . time away from work . . . varies in different parts of the world. In France, workers get five to six weeks of paid vacation. Sweden has the most vacation time of a European country at eight weeks. In the United States, vacation time for most workers is limited to two weeks. In Japan, three weeks is offered, but reports show that only half of this time is actually used. For example, in 1990, 15.5 days of vacation were given in Japan, but only 8.2 days were taken.

**Make predictions**

See page 8

**C.** Before the lecture, think about everything you have learned and discussed about the pace of life. What do you expect to learn from the lecture? Write three predictions below. Compare your predictions with a partner.

1. _____

2. _____

3. _____

**Watch the lecture**

**GO ONLINE**

*chapter 2*

**D.** Watch the lecture, and take notes in your notebook. Remember to write down the most important words. Include information about the following ideas.

• Topic of the lecture

• Pace of life

• Factors looked at in the study

• Fastest countries

• Slowest countries

• Factors that make pace of life faster

**Assess your comprehension**

**E.** Check the statement that best describes how well you were able to understand the lecture.

____ I was able to understand all the ideas in the lecture.

____ I was able to understand most of the ideas in the lecture.

____ I was able to understand only a few of the ideas in the lecture.

**F.** Use your notes to answer these questions.

**1.** Why did Professor Levine want to conduct the study?

_____

_____

_____

**2.** What three factors did the researchers look at and assess?

_____

_____

_____

**3.** What are the places where life is fastest? And slowest?

_____

_____

_____

**4.** What are five factors that places with the fastest pace have in common?

_____

_____

_____

NOTE-TAKING STRATEGY

### Summarize the Lecture

A good way to help remember a lecture is to put the key ideas into your own words. This will also help you know that you understood all the information and that your notes are complete.

As soon as possible after a lecture, put the key ideas into your own words, and speak them out loud to a study partner or to yourself.

Imagine this situation: Your friend had to miss class because she was ill. The next day, she asks you to tell her quickly what the professor said in the lecture. What would you tell her to give her the idea of the lecture?

- the topic of the lecture
- the big picture of the lecture (the most important ideas)
- a few important points and examples

This is the same information that you use when you summarize.

### Expressions for Summarizing

- The professor talked about . . .
- He said that . . .
- And then he discussed . . .
- He gave two good examples of . . .
- She explained . . .
- After that, he wrapped up with . . .
- She told us . . .

List more examples  **G.** Work with a partner to think of other expressions for summarizing. Write your examples here.

_____

_____

_____

Summarize the lecture  **H.** Review your notes from the lecture. Then summarize the main points of the lecture for your partner. Take turns, and talk for 2–3 minutes only.

**ACADEMIC DISCUSSION STRATEGY**

### Lead the Group Discussion

During a group discussion, it can be difficult for the group to know how and when to begin the discussion. Assigning a group leader to manage the group can help. Choose a discussion leader who begins the discussion and gives everyone a chance to talk.

**Expressions for Leading the Group Discussion**

- Is everybody ready to start?
- Let's start with question number 1.
- Anna, do you want to begin?
- Marino, what do you think about that?
- Has everyone had a chance to speak?
- Any other comments?
- Thanks, everyone. Good discussion.

**List more examples**

**A.** Work with a partner to think of other expressions for leading a group discussion. Write your examples here.

_____

_____

_____

**Practice leading the group discussion**

**B.** In a group, read and discuss the questions. For each question, choose a different discussion leader to begin the discussion, and make sure that each person in the group participates.

1. What are your general impressions of the pace of life in a small town?

2. What are your general impressions of the pace of life in a big city?

3. What are the advantages and disadvantages of living in a fast- or slow-paced area?

**C.** Discuss these ideas with your classmates. Remember to use the
expressions for leading the group discussion.

1. If a study of pace was done in the city you live in, would your city be
   ranked fast, medium, or slow? Give specific examples of behavior you
   have seen in the post office, with clocks, and walking speed. What other
   behavior would you add to the list?

2. Where have the different people in your group lived in their lives?
   Compare the pace of life in the different countries, cities, or towns.

3. The lecture says that strong economies and a lot of industrialization
   lead to a faster pace of life. Why do you think this is true?

4. Look back at your notes. What was another idea in the lecture that
   you found important or interesting? Tell the class why you think it is
   important or interesting. Ask for your classmates' opinions.

**PRESENTATION STRATEGY**

**Use Your Hands Effectively**

Speakers often aren't sure what to do with their hands when they give a presentation. They may use their hands too much or too little. Sometimes they move their hands in ways that don't match what they are saying. As a result, they may distract the audience. The audience might focus on the speaker's hands instead of the ideas in the presentation.

Use your hands in ways that keep the audience focused on your ideas. Your hand movements should help your audience follow what you are saying.

**Check your comprehension**

 **ONLINE**

**A.** Watch a student give a presentation about her observations of the pace of life in two parts of a city. Answer these two questions.

1. What city did the student observe?

   _____

2. What did the student measure?

   _____

**Notice hand use**

**GO ONLINE**

**B.** Watch the video again. Think about the information in the strategy box above. List two problems with the way the student uses her hands.

_____

_____

**GO ONLINE** **C.** The student received some suggestions on her presentation and delivered it again. Watch the new presentation. In your notebook, list two improvements the student made to the way she used her hands.

**PRESENTATION STRATEGY**

**Effective Hand Use While Giving a Presentation**
- Don't play with things such as coins, pens, or notecards.
- Use an appropriate number of gestures—not too many, not too few.
- Use gestures that match your ideas. For example, if you say, "It's very big," your gesture could be holding your arms and hands wide apart.

**List more examples**  **D.** Work with a partner to think of other examples of effective hand use. Write your examples in your notebook.

**Practice effective hand use**  **E.** Work in a group. Choose one sentence below, and think about the idea it communicates. Then stand in front of your group and read the sentence. Have each student in the group take a turn with a different sentence. Practice the strategies for effective hand use.

1. There are three things that I love about cities.

2. I want to compare Switzerland with Japan.

3. Some of the streets in Paris are wide, and some are very narrow.

4. The pace of life in many countries has increased in the last ten years.

After you finish, have your classmates give you feedback on your hand gestures. Ask them these two questions:

1. What are two ways I used my hands effectively?

2. What is one way to improve how I use my hands?

**Give a presentation**  **F.** Develop and deliver a presentation about the pace of life in two parts of your town or city.

Choose two local places that you think have a different pace of life. For example, you can choose a university campus and the downtown area of your city. Then observe how people move in those places. For example, notice how fast they walk or how long it takes to buy a cup of coffee or a stamp.

Present your observations to your class. Explain whether you think the two places have a similar pace or a different pace. Use the strategy for using your hands effectively.

Before you prepare your presentation, review the ideas and vocabulary from this chapter.

**A.** Work in a group. Follow the steps to analyze a course syllabus.

Look through the course syllabus of one of your courses, or go online and find a course syllabus in a field of study that interests your group.

**Take Notes**

Look carefully at the syllabus you choose. Take notes about the course components, objectives, grading policy, and class requirements.

**Discuss the Course**

- What will the course cover?

- Which course topics are most interesting to the group? Why?

- What does the professor consider to be the most important requirements? How do you know?

Remember to show interest during the discussion.

**Present What You Learn**

Present the information to your class. Remember to use good posture, good eye contact, and effective hand use.

**B.** Work in a group. Develop a guide for visitors to your country. Give advice about what visitors should know about how the people in your culture use their time.

**Discuss the Topic**

- What is the appropriate time to arrive for an appointment with a professor?

- What is the appropriate time to arrive for dinner with friends?

- For the above, should people be exactly on time, or can they arrive late? That is, how late is acceptable in your culture?

- What is your culture's tradition for waiting in line?

- Is there an orderly procedure for waiting in line, or do people push ahead?

Discuss another aspect of time and pace that is important for understanding your culture.

**Take Notes**

Take notes during your group's discussion. Use this information to create the guide.

**Present Your Knowledge**

Present the information to your class. Remember to use good posture, good eye contact, and effective hand use.

# Unit Goals

UNIT
2

## CHAPTER 3

**Learn how successful companies get ideas for their products**

### Listening Strategy
• Recognize lecture language that signals the topic

### Note-Taking Strategy
• Use an informal outline to take notes

### Academic Discussion Strategy
• Learn expressions for entering a discussion

### Presentation Strategy
• Catch your audience's attention with a greeting and a poll at the beginning of your presentation

## CHAPTER 4

**Learn about global brands and business plans**

### Listening Strategy
• Recognize lecture language that signals the big picture

### Note-Taking Strategy
• Leave space in your notes to add information later

### Academic Discussion Strategy
• Contribute ideas to the discussion

### Presentation Strategy
• Use signals to transition to new parts of the presentation

# Business

business \\'bɪznəs\\ The study of making, buying, selling, or supplying goods or services for money

**Think about the topic** **A.** Look at the pictures. Then work with a partner to answer the questions.

1. Which of the products is the most interesting to you?
   *iphones*
2. How do you think the company got the idea for the product?
   *I think the got the idea to make life easier*
3. Imagine that you are the president of a company. You want to design a new product (an electronics product, a game, or a piece of kitchen equipment) that young people will enjoy. What kind of people would you hire to create the new product?
   *I will hire 18 years old people*

**B.** Read this article about two people who help companies design new products.

# Meet the Innovation Experts

Meet two of today's most successful experts in business **innovation**. What do they have in common? They both know how to **think outside the box** and create success after success.

## Beth Comstock, General Electric Company

"I'm propelled by curiosity," says Beth Comstock, senior vice president and chief marketing officer of General Electric. GE is most famous for its electric appliances, but the company also makes medical equipment, electric motors, and much more. In 2003, the company's **CEO** decided that GE needed more innovation. He wanted the people in charge of creating GE **products** to take **risks** in their thinking.

To achieve this task, the CEO put Beth Comstock in charge of making GE and its 300,000 workers more creative and innovative. One of Comstock's innovations was the dreaming workshop. In dreaming workshops, product designers and **customers** came together to talk about products that only existed in people's imaginations. Comstock later introduced a company-wide network called ecomagination. Ecomagination used new technology to reduce environmental impact. Comstock was also responsible for a network called healthymagination. It used innovation to improve people's health. Beth Comstock's out-of-the-box thinking has produced many new ideas for GE.

## Sohrab Vossoughi, ZIBA Design

Combining research with design is a key to business innovation. For that reason, it is not surprising that Sohrab Vossoughi won 200 design awards for his company. As CEO of ZIBA Design, Sohrab Vossoughi developed a new product design **strategy**. He wanted to give customers a very emotional experience when they bought the products he designed. His way of thinking created big **profits** for his company and for the companies that paid for his ideas.

When a giant electronic hardware company hired ZIBA to design headsets for cell phones, Vossoughi developed a winning solution. His research showed that most people prefer headsets that they can touch and use without thinking. They also wanted headsets that look good near their faces. Vossoughi worked with his design team to develop scenarios of possible users. For example, one type of user was the Teenage Talker. This type of user spends hours on the phone each night talking with friends. Another type of user was the Family Connector. A Family Connector calls everyone in the family each weekend. Vossoughi's research led to a variety of new headsets. These headsets helped the electronic hardware company expand the **market** for its products. Thanks to Vossoughi, the headsets became a huge success with customers of all ages.

**C.** With a partner, discuss these questions about the reading.

1. What innovations was Beth Comstock responsible for?

2. How did Sohrab Vossoughi make people want to buy the products he helped to design?

3. What are the similarities between the two people described in the article?

**D.** Match the words from the reading with their definitions. Look back at the reading on page 29 to check your answers.

_g_ 1. innovation  **a.** a plan that is used to achieve a goal

_d_ 2. CEO  **b.** something that is made in a factory or grown

_e_ 3. risk  **c.** a group of people who might buy something

_h_ 4. customer  **d.** Chief Executive Officer: the highest person in a company

_b_ 5. product  **e.** a possibility that something bad might happen

_a_ 6. strategy  **f.** the money that you make from selling something

_f_ 7. profit  **g.** a new idea, invention, or way of doing something

_c_ 8. market  **h.** a person who buys something

**E.** Circle the phrase with a similar meaning to the underlined idiom.

Some companies can be successful using traditional ways of creating new products, but other companies are successful when they <u>think outside the box</u>.

**a.** don't spend much money

**b.** think in a new and different way

**c.** work very quickly with fewer people

**F.** Discuss these questions in a group. Share your answers with the class.

1. Was it a good idea for GE to hire Beth Comstock? Why or why not?

2. If you were the CEO of a company, would you hire people like Beth Comstock and Sohrab Vossoughi? Why or why not? What other kinds of people would you hire to think of new products?

**G.** With a partner, discuss three things that you have learned from the reading and from your discussion about product innovation.

1. _____

2. _____

3. _____

**Prepare for the listening strategy**

**H.** To help you understand the listening strategy, discuss the situation below with a partner. Then answer the questions.

Nadia works at a restaurant in the morning and then goes directly to school. Because of this, she arrives a few minutes late to the lecture.

She says that she has trouble following the professor during the lecture. Her friends get to class on time and say the professor is easy to follow.

What information does Nadia miss when she arrives late? Why is it important to hear the beginning of a lecture?

**LISTENING STRATEGY**

**Recognize Lecture Language That Signals the Topic**

In any university course, a professor lectures every day about the subject of the course.

Every course subject has many topics within it. For example, in a course on international business, a professor lectures on topics such as countries, people, finance, and international products. When a student listens to a lecture, the most important thing the student needs to know is what the lecture is about. The professor usually states the topic, or what the lecture is going to be about, at the beginning of the lecture.

Listen for the words and expressions that professors use to tell you the topic.

**Expressions That Signal the Topic of a Lecture**
- Our topic today is . . .
- I want to talk about . . .
- I'm going to talk about . . .
- We're going to discuss . . .
- What I want to talk about today is . . .
- Today I'm going to focus on . . .

**List more examples**

**I.** Work with a partner to think of other expressions that signal the topic of a lecture. Write your examples here.

_____

_____

_____

**J.** Read these introductions to two business lectures. Then do the
following:

- Circle the topic.
- Underline and label the lecture language that signals the topic.

1. Greetings, everyone. I'm excited about today's lecture. We're going to
   discuss innovation. . . . That's right . . . how businesses get new ideas,
   who thinks of the ideas, and what they do with them. Are you ready?

2. Good morning. Last week, we talked about how important innovation is
   to our economy. But who are the innovators? Well, today I'm going to
   focus on the personality characteristics of several famous innovators.

**K.** Listen to the introductions of three different lectures on innovation.
First, listen to each introduction. Then write down the lecture language
that signals the topic and the topic.

1. Topic lecture language: Software Innovation our topic
   Today is
   Topic: Different stwark = New Idea banking s
   Bussines s - were going to discus.

   *[handwritten in margin: S → men softwere]*

2. Topic lecture language: what I want to talk about, I am go
   Tusday productinnava in new car
   Topic: I goinng to cover develofment.

3. Topic lecture language: we're going to discuss Innovation
   in Food word.
   Topic: will look at alist

**L.** Study the meaning of these general academic words. Fill in the blanks
with the correct words in the correct form.

**type:** a group of people or things that are similar
**in fact:** a phrase that is used to emphasize a point or to add a
factual example

General Electric makes many _____ of electric products.

_____, it makes over 100 kinds of products just for

the kitchen.

**NOTE-TAKING STRATEGY**

## Use an Informal Outline

Your notes should give you an accurate record of a lecture's ideas and organization. To show how ideas relate to each other, write the most important ideas close to the left margin. Add related details below and to the right. This is called *indentation*. It will give you a clear view of the lecture organization.

The following is an excerpt from a lecture on innovation and a student's informal outline.

> I want to talk about innovation in the skin-care business. And I want to discuss two ways that skin-care companies are using innovation to create new products. One, they are creating an experience for the customer. Two, they're bringing "real people" into the company and watching how they react to new products. A good example of this technique is at the Softcare Company.

| Innovation in skin-care business—2 ways |
| --- |
| create experience for customer |
| bring "real people" into company |
| good example: Softcare |

**Analyze the notes**

**A.** Use the transcript and student notes above to answer these questions in your notebook.

1. How did the student show what the topic is?

2. How did the student show the ways that the companies use innovation?

3. How did the student indicate that Softcare is related to the second point?

**Take notes using an informal outline**

**B.** Read this excerpt from a lecture on innovation in electronics. Take notes in your notebook using an informal outline.

> Let's talk about product innovation in electronics. Some examples of these kinds of products are digital music players, cameras, and computer hardware. In the world of computer hardware, there's one company I want to focus on—it's Logitech. This company makes headsets, computer keyboards, and the mouse for your computer.

**C.** Before the lecture, think about everything you have learned and discussed about innovation. What do you expect to learn from the lecture? Write three predictions below. Compare your predictions with a partner.

1. _____

2. _____

3. _____

**D.** Watch the lecture, and take notes using an informal outline. Remember to listen for the lecture language that signals the topic.

Topic:

Innovation in the past:

Innovation in the present:

What innovative companies have in common:

Successful companies:

**E.** Check the statement that best describes how well you were able to
understand the lecture language.

___ I was able to recognize when the lecturer said the topic.

___ I didn't recognize when the lecturer said the topic.

**F.** Use your notes to answer these questions.

**1.** How did companies create new products in the past?

_____

_____

_____

**2.** What are two things that innovative companies today have in common?

_____

_____

_____

**3.** How did Apple come up with the idea for the iPod?

_____

_____

_____

_____

**4.** How did Starbucks use innovative thinking to bring in new customers?

_____

_____

_____

_____

**G.** Were you able to answer the questions in Exercise F using the
information in your notes? Compare and discuss your notes with a few
other students. Help each other fill in any missing information. Revise
your notes.

**H.** Work with a partner. Review your notes from the lecture. Then
summarize the main points of the lecture for your partner. Take turns,
and talk for 2–3 minutes only.

**ACADEMIC DISCUSSION STRATEGY**

### Enter the Discussion

Your professors will often ask you to discuss the ideas in the lecture with the whole class or with a group of classmates. The professor will expect all students to participate actively in class discussions. Don't wait for someone to ask you to speak. Instead, use expressions to enter the discussion, so you can share your ideas.

### Expressions for Entering the Discussion

- I'd like to say something here.
- Can I add something to that?
- Can I say something here?

**Note:** Speakers often say a small word or interjection to get attention before using one of the expressions above.

- Well, . . . I'd like to say something here.
- Um, . . . can I add something to that?
- So, . . . could I say something here?

**List more examples**  **A.** Work with a partner to think of other expressions for entering a discussion. Write your examples here.

_____

_____

_____

_____

**B.** In a group, read and discuss the questions. Keep the conversation going until every student has had a chance to practice entering the discussion. Use your own ideas or the ones given below.

1. What are some of your favorite new products, and why do you like them? Explain your answer in detail.

   **Possible Ideas**
   smartphones
   cameras
   headphones

2. Imagine that you are looking for a job as a product innovator. What kind of company would you try to work in? Why?

   **Possible Ideas**
   a financial company
   a health-care company
   a computer company

**C.** Discuss these ideas with your classmates. Remember to use the expressions for entering the discussion.

1. Should companies take risks when they think of new products? What are some of the advantages and disadvantages of taking risks?

2. What kind of strategy mentioned in the lecture would you like to try? How would you use this strategy? Explain your answer in detail.

3. Is thinking outside the box always the best way to create new product designs? Why or why not? What are the possible negative effects of always thinking outside the box?

4. Look back at your notes. What was another idea in the lecture that you found important or interesting? Tell the class why you think it is important or interesting. Ask for your classmates' opinions.

**PRESENTATION STRATEGY**

**Catch the Audience's Attention**

A good speaker begins a presentation with a quick and friendly greeting. This makes the audience feel welcome. Then the speaker must catch the audience's attention so they will be interested and curious.

One way speakers catch the audience's attention is by taking a poll. They ask a quick question that the audience can answer by raising their hands. By participating in this way, the audience becomes more involved in the topic.

Catch your audience's attention by taking a poll at the beginning of your presentation.

**Check your comprehension**

**A.** Watch a student give a presentation about a company and one of its innovations. Answer these two questions.

**1.** What kind of products does the company make?

_____

**2.** What innovation does the speaker describe?

_____

**Notice how the speaker catches the audience's attention**

**B.** Watch the video again. Think about the information in the strategy box above. List two problems with the way the speaker connects with the audience.

_____

_____

_____

_____

 **C.** The student received some suggestions about her presentation and delivered it again. Watch the new presentation. List two improvements the student made to the way she connects with the audience.

_____

_____

_____

_____

**Expressions for Taking a Poll**
- How many of you have ever seen . . . ?
- Raise your hand if you have ever heard of . . .
- How many of you have experienced . . . ?

**Note:** After you ask your questions, give the audience time to raise their hands to answer. Be sure to briefly summarize what you notice in their answers.

---

**List more examples**

**D.** Work with a partner to think of other ways to take a poll that catches the audience's attention. Write your examples in your notebook.

---

**Practice catching attention**

*we start*
*Today I want to*
*Take about ....*

**E.** Stand in front of a group of classmates. Deliver the beginning of a presentation in which you describe an everyday product, such as a toothbrush, a cell phone, or a kitchen tool. Use the strategy for catching the audience's attention.

After you finish, have your group give you feedback on how well you caught their attention. Ask them these two questions:

**1.** In what way did I catch your attention?

**2.** What is one way to improve how I catch the audience's attention?

---

**Give a presentation**

**F.** Develop and deliver a presentation about a company and one of its innovations.

Choose a company, and research where it is located, what it produces, and its innovations. Present your research to your class.

Use the strategy for catching your audience's attention.

Before you prepare your presentation, review the ideas and vocabulary from this chapter.

# CHAPTER 4  Global Business: The Case of MTV

**Listen and Apply New Strategies**

**Think about the topic**

**A.** Look at the collage of international brands. Then work with a partner to answer the questions below.

1. What types of products do these brands represent?

2. Where can people find these products?

3. Where are these products most popular? Why?

4. Is there anywhere that people cannot find these products? Why or why not?

5. MTV is a very successful brand that many young people know and enjoy. Why is it so successful?

6. Which products appeal more to businesspeople? Which appeal to women? Which appeal to men?

**B.** Read this article about international brands.

# Global Brands

Which **brands** are the most successful around the world? Every year business magazines and Web sites make lists of the top 100 international brands. To get on the list, a brand must earn over $1 billion and over a third of its profits must come from outside its home country.

### Top 20 Brands

| | |
|---|---|
| 1. Coca-Cola | 11. Toyota |
| 2. IBM | 12. Mercedes-Benz |
| 3. Microsoft | 13. Cisco |
| 4. Google | 14. Nokia |
| 5. GE | 15. BMW |
| 6. McDonald's | 16. Gillette |
| 7. Intel | 17. Samsung |
| 8. Apple | 18. Louis Vutton |
| 9. Disney | 19. Honda |
| 10. Hewlett-Packard | 20. Oracle |

Brands like McDonald's, Mercedes-Benz, and Nokia are familiar to people all over the world. They are **global** brands.

Companies with some of the most **popular** international brands are finding new customers and increasing their profits with a simple idea: they create one image for their brand all over the world. In this type of **business plan**, a brand has one name and one "look" wherever it is sold. Companies do not change the brand to fit the **local** area.

An excellent **case study** is Samsung, an electronics company from Korea. Until the 1990s, Samsung was making inexpensive electronics under many different brands— Wiseview, Tantus, Yepp, and others. These brands were successful in their own local areas, but the different names caused problems for the company. Samsung **invested** in creating better-quality products, and it put the same brand name, Samsung, on all of them. The company thought that if customers liked one Samsung product, they might buy another Samsung product.

Beginning in 2001, the "new" Samsung began selling high-quality cell phones and digital televisions. Soon people began to think of Samsung as a very high-quality brand. As a result, ten years later, Samsung rose to number 17 on *Bloomberg Businessweek* magazine's list of the top 100 international brands. This **statistic** says it all: Samsung's profits went up nearly 200 percent. For Samsung, like many other international companies, a strong "global brand" was the key to success. These companies are now **at the top of their game** and hope to stay there.

**C.** With a partner, discuss these questions about the reading.

1. How does a brand get on the list of the top 100 international brands?

2. How are some companies finding new customers and increasing their profits?

3. What problem did Samsung have? How did it solve the problem?

**D.** Circle the answer that correctly completes the definition of the underlined words. Look back at the reading on page 41 to check your answers.

1. A <u>brand</u> is the _____ of a product that is made by a particular company.

   **a.** name    **b.** profit

2. When a product is <u>global</u>, it is known in most areas of the _____.

   **a.** world    **b.** business

3. Something is <u>popular</u> when many people _____ it.

   **a.** see    **b.** like

4. A <u>business plan</u> explains what a company wants to do in the _____.

   **a.** future    **b.** present

5. Something is <u>local</u> when it is _____ the area where you live.

   **a.** far away from    **b.** connected to

6. A <u>case study</u> is _____ a particular thing or situation in order to help people understand a larger idea.

   **a.** a careful examination of    **b.** a funny story about

7. When companies <u>invest</u> in something, they _____ money on it and hope to get something good in return.

   **a.** save    **b.** spend

8. A <u>statistic</u> is a _____ that represents facts or measurements.

   **a.** number    **b.** person

**E.** Circle the phrase with a similar meaning to the underlined idiom.

When companies are <u>at the top of their game</u>, they _____.

**a.** play a lot of sports   **b.** are very successful   **c.** need to work harder

**F.** Discuss these questions in a group. Share your answers with the class.

1. Is Samsung's business plan a good idea for other companies? Why or why not?

2. Do you think MTV uses a business plan that is similar to Samsung's?

**G.** With a partner, discuss three things that you have learned from the reading and from your discussion about global brands.

1. _____

2. _____

3. _____

**Recognize Lecture Language That Signals the Big Picture**

At the beginning of a lecture, the professor usually tells you the big picture, the general plan of the lecture.

The big picture is like a map for students to follow. It shows how the professor will present the material in the lecture.

Listen for the words and expressions that professors use to tell you the big picture of the lecture.

**Expressions That Signal the Big Picture**

- First we'll look at . . . and then we'll look at . . .
- I'm going to cover . . . and then . . .
- We'll discuss a few examples of/types of . . .
- Today I'm going to look at several ways that . . .
- I want to discuss the causes . . .
- What I want to do is compare . . . to . . .

**H.** Work with a partner to think of other expressions that signal the big picture. Write your examples here.

_____

_____

_____

**I.** Read this introduction from a lecture on global brands. Then do the following:
- Circle the topic.
- Underline and label the lecture language that signals the big picture.

Hi there, everyone. It's nine o'clock, so let's go ahead and get started. What I want to talk about this morning is the history of global brands. Now, why do I want to talk about the history of global brands? Shouldn't we be talking about the future? Maybe, but in business, we can't understand the future until we understand the past. . . . All right. I want to discuss the causes of the failure of some companies that have tried to do business—Novalites and other companies that are no longer around.

**J.** Listen to the introductions of two different lectures. Listen for the lecture language that signals the topic, and write down the topic. Then listen to each introduction again, and write down the big picture lecture language.

1. Topic lecture language: _____

_____

Topic: _____

_____

Big picture lecture language: _____

_____

2. Topic lecture language: _____

_____

Topic: _____

_____

Big picture lecture language: _____

_____

Learn general academic words

**K.** Study the meaning of these general academic words. Fill in the blanks below with the correct words in the correct form. Compare your answers with a partner.

**in general:** usually, in most situations

**result:** something that happens or exists because of something else

To sell their products in other countries, companies need to have a good business plan. If they are not prepared, the _____ can be very bad for the company and all of their brands. When we look at case studies, we can see that, _____, companies that have a solid business plan for international sales are more successful.

**NOTE-TAKING STRATEGY**

### Leave Space in Your Informal Outline

The purpose of taking notes is to give you an accurate record of a lecture. This helps you to study later. While taking notes, leave space between notes of important ideas. This will help you see the important ideas and add more information to your notes after the lecture.

The following is an excerpt from a lecture and one student's notes from the lecture.

| Excerpt | Notes |
|---|---|
| **Samsung really wanted to find new global markets. So they did two things. They gave all their products the same brand name—Samsung. For example, Tantus became Samsung. So did Yepp. The second thing they did was they invested in better quality products.   And so . . . when they re-branded and improved their quality, their profits increased nearly 200 percent.** | Samsung wanted new global markets<br><br>Did 2 things<br><br>• Gave all products same name<br><br>    Tantus<br><br>    Yepp<br><br><br>• Invested in better quality products<br><br><br>Result: Profits increased 200% |

**Analyze the notes**

**A.** Look at the excerpt and notes above. With a partner, discuss these questions.

**1.** What are some important ideas in this section of the notes?

**2.** After the lecture, where could the student add extra information?

**Leave space in your notes**

**B.** Read this excerpt from a lecture on global brands. Take notes in your notebook. Leave space in your notes between important ideas.

**There are at least two ways global brands are increasing their profits. Many of the most successful international brands have one "look" all over the world. So, for example, we have eBay. eBay uses the same Web site in every country where it does business. Another way is to use the same advertisements in every country. Look at the company Global Banks. It started using the same ads all over the world, and the value of its brand went up 20 percent.**

**Make predictions**

See page 8

**C.** Before the lecture, think about everything you have learned and discussed about global brands. What do you expect to learn from the lecture? Write three predictions below. Compare your predictions with a partner.

1. _____

2. _____

3. _____

**Watch the lecture**

**GO ONLINE**

**D.** Watch the lecture, and take notes, leaving space between important ideas. Remember to listen for the lecture language that signals the topic and big picture.

Topic:

Statistics on MTV:

Profits:

Factors in MTV's success:

Result:

**E.** Check the statement that best describes how well you were able to
understand lecture language.

_____ I was able to recognize when the lecturer signaled the big picture
of the lecture.

_____ I didn't recognize when the lecturer signaled the big picture of
the lecture.

**F.** Use your notes to answer these questions.

**1.** What are some of the statistics that show how successful MTV is around
the world?

_____

_____

_____

**2.** What is MTV's business plan?

_____

_____

_____

**3.** What are two things that MTV does to be successful?

_____

_____

_____

**4.** What does MTV do to produce programs with local talent?

_____

_____

_____

**G.** Were you able to answer the questions in Exercise F using the
information in your notes? Compare and discuss your notes with a few
other students. Help each other fill in any missing information. Revise
your notes.

**H.** Work with a partner. Review your notes from the lecture. Then
summarize the main points of the lecture for your partner. Take turns,
and talk for 2–3 minutes only.

**ACADEMIC DISCUSSION STRATEGY**

### Contribute Your Ideas to the Discussion

Adding your ideas to classroom discussions shows that you understand the topic and are interested. Your ideas might be points from the lecture that you think are interesting, comments about the topic, or your own opinions. Use expressions to show that you want to contribute something to the discussion.

**Expressions for Contributing Ideas to the Discussion**
- I think . . .
- In my opinion, . . .
- I noticed that . . .
- I think it was interesting that . . .
- . . . is really important because . . .

List more examples

**A.** Work with a partner to think of other expressions used for contributing to a discussion. Write your examples here.

_____

_____

_____

**B.** In a group, read and discuss the questions. Keep the conversation going until every student has had a chance to practice contributing to the discussion. Use your own ideas or the ones given below.

**1.** What are your favorite global brands, and why do you like them?

> **Possible Ideas**
> Starbucks
> Nokia
> BMW

**2.** Why do you watch MTV or other music channels?

> **Possible Ideas**
> to see my favorite stars
> to learn about the latest fashions

**C.** Discuss these ideas with your classmates. Remember to use the expressions for contributing your ideas to the discussion.

**1.** What if MTV used Samsung's business plan and had one "look" and one style all over the world? What would happen to MTV?

**2.** Imagine the CEO of MTV needs your advice about ways to increase the brand's international profits. What would you tell the CEO of MTV?

**3.** Choose a brand from the list of the top 20 global brands in the article on page 41. What business plan would you use for this global brand?

**4.** Look back at your notes. What was another idea in the lecture that you found important or interesting? Tell the class why you think it is important or interesting. Ask for your classmates' opinions.

**PRESENTATION STRATEGY**

**Signal a Transition**

During a presentation, the audience needs to be able to follow as the speaker moves from one idea to the next idea. The speaker should guide the audience. Speakers do this by using expressions to clearly signal what idea will come next in the presentation. These expressions are called *transitions*.

Use transitions to help the audience follow you when you change from one idea to the next.

**Check your comprehension**

**A.** Watch a student give a presentation about a product that is sold internationally. Answer these two questions.

**1.** What is the product?

_____

**2.** Where would this student like to market the product?

_____

**Notice transitions**

**B.** Watch the video again. Think about the information in the strategy box above. How do the student's transitions help you follow the presentation?

_____

_____

**PRESENTATION STRATEGY**

**Expressions for Signaling a Transition**
- Now that I've told you about . . . I'm going to explain . . .
- I'd like to move on to . . .
- Let me turn to . . .

**List more examples**

**C.** Work with a partner to think of other expressions for signaling a transition. Write your examples here.

_____

_____

_____

**D.** Stand in front of a group of classmates. Tell your group about one of your favorite possessions such as a hat, a book, or a souvenir. Describe the possession. Then tell how you acquired the item. Finally, explain why it is important to you. Use transitions to signal when you move from one idea to a different idea.

After you finish, have your classmates give you feedback on your transitions. Ask them these two questions:

**1.** What are two ways I used transitions effectively?

**2.** What is one way to improve my transitions?

**E.** Develop and deliver a presentation about marketing a product.

*Canvas*

Choose a product, and develop a plan for how the company should market the product in your country.

- Describe the product.

- Explain the habits of the people in your country that relate to the product. For example, for a food product, describe eating habits of the people in your country so that marketers can understand their market.

- Explain how the company can market the product to appeal to people in your country.

- Give your opinion about how the product might sell in your country.

Use the strategy for signaling transitions in ideas.

Before you prepare your presentation, review the ideas and vocabulary from this chapter.

**A.** Work in a group. Research business innovators.

Go online to research business innovators. Look for people who have developed innovative products, ideas, or processes. Choose one person you find interesting. Then do further research on that person and his or her innovations.

**Take Notes**
Take notes about the person's life, education, professional background, and the innovation that has made the person famous.

**Discuss Your Research**
Discuss how the innovator's personal and professional background might have helped the person in his or her career. Discuss how the innovation has affected other people. Give everyone in the group an opportunity to enter and contribute to the discussion.

**Present What You Learn**
Present the information to your class. Remember to be friendly as you speak. Consider using a poll to get your audience's attention.

**B.** Work in a group. Follow the steps to develop a business plan for a global business.

Think of a local company that everyone knows (a restaurant, clothing store, small manufacturer, etc.). Imagine you are the new owners. You want to turn the local business into a global business.

**Listen and Take Notes**
Determine who the market is for the business. Develop a survey for this market. Ask questions about what people like and dislike about the business. Ask how the business can better serve its customers. Ask for suggestions on how the business might expand into new markets. Take notes of all the responses.

**Discuss the Results**
Work with others in your group to develop a plan for advertising your business. Consider what countries you would market to and how to advertise. Consider the business's name. Should it change? Why?

**Present Your Conclusions**
Present your business plan to the class. Remember to use transitions as you present different parts of your business plan.

# Unit Goals

**UNIT**

**3**

## CHAPTER 5

**Learn about how celebrity news is changing the media**

### Listening Strategy
- Recognize lecture language that signals a transition

### Note-Taking Strategy
- Use symbols instead of words in your notes

### Academic Discussion Strategy
- Interrupt and ask for clarification during the discussion

### Presentation Strategy
- Create rapport with your audience

## CHAPTER 6

**Learn about three revolutions in mass communication**

### Listening Strategy
- Recognize lecture language that signals a definition

### Note-Taking Strategy
- Use abbreviations instead of full words in your notes

### Academic Discussion Strategy
- Ask for more information during the discussion

### Presentation Strategy
- Open the floor to questions to connect with your audience

# Media Studies

media studies \ˈmidiə ˈstʌdiz\ The study of the processes by which information is exchanged

**Listen and Apply New Strategies**

**Think about the topic**  **A.** Look at the picture of a celebrity, reporters, and fans. Then work with a partner to answer the questions below.

1. Think about your favorite singer, movie star, and athlete. What information do you know about each person? How did you find out this information?

2. Why are people interested in famous people?

3. Why would a person want to be famous? What benefits come with fame?

4. What are some of the drawbacks of fame?

5. Would you want to be famous? Why or why not?

**B.** Read this article about the growing interest in celebrities.

# Celebrities in the Media:
# Are You Starstruck?

*"People in our society today are focused too much on celebrities and all the activities of people in the entertainment world."*

Many people would agree with this statement by James Houran, a psychologist with the Southern Illinois School of Medicine. He and a group of researchers interviewed over 600 people to try to understand our intense interest in famous people. They discovered three categories of "**celebrity** interest":

- **Entertainment** Social: People in this category have a mild interest in celebrities. For example, with their friends they might discuss the recent marriage of a famous movie star just for fun.
- Intense Personal: People in this category seem to feel that they have a special connection with a celebrity. Such a person might say, "David Beckham is a good friend of mine," even though it is not true.
- Celebrity Sickness: Here, the interest in celebrities is so great that it is unhealthy, a kind of sickness. A person in this category might say, "When Aishwarya Rai reads my love letters, she's going to fall in love with me."

The researchers learned that a third of the people interviewed fit into the last category. Houran's team says that this unhealthy interest in celebrities is caused by the increase in entertainment news in the **mass media**, in both **print** and **broadcast** media. It is just one example of the effect the media have on people's lives today.

"People have been interested in celebrities for as long as there have been famous people," says Houran. But this interest has become much stronger with the increase in media **coverage** of celebrities. The Internet has increased the amount of entertainment **content** that we now have access to. In fact, people no longer have to look through newspapers, magazines, or other traditional news **sources** for stories of their favorite celebrities. They can now use the Internet to find all the latest information on any star they choose. So, **in a nutshell**, it seems that the more media choices we have, the crazier we become about celebrities.

**C.** With a partner, discuss these questions about the reading.

1. Who is James Houran, and what did he do?

2. What percentage of the people interviewed have celebrity sickness?

3. Why are more and more people interested in celebrities now?

**D.** Match the words from the reading with their definitions. Look back at the reading on page 55 to check your answers.

_____ **1.** celebrity

    **a.** a TV show, book, newspaper, etc., that gives you information about something

_____ **2.** entertainment

    **b.** writing that is in books and newspapers

_____ **3.** mass media

    **c.** a famous person, usually an actor, singer, or sports star

_____ **4.** print

    **d.** things such as movies and television shows that people watch for fun

_____ **5.** broadcast

    **e.** the amount of reporting about something on TV, on the radio, or in newspapers

_____ **6.** coverage

    **f.** something that is sent out on radio or television

_____ **7.** content

    **g.** all the organizations such as newspapers and TV that provide news and information to many people

_____ **8.** source

    **h.** the words or ideas in a television program, book, article, etc.

**E.** Circle the phrase with a similar meaning to the underlined idiom.

The professor spent 15 minutes explaining the meaning of the word _celebrity_. <u>In a nutshell</u>, it means "a famous person."

**a.** said simply

**b.** however

**c.** over a long time

**F.** Discuss these questions in a group. Share your answers with the class.

**1.** Which category of "celebrity interest" are you in? Explain your answer. Do you know someone who has intense personal interest in a celebrity? If so, give some examples of his or her behavior.

**2.** What are some other reasons that people might be very interested in celebrities?

**G.** With a partner, discuss three things that you have learned from the reading and from your discussion about celebrities in the news.

1. _____

2. _____

3. _____

### Recognize Lecture Language That Signals a Transition

In Chapters 3 and 4, you learned that professors usually tell you at the beginning of a lecture how information will be organized. During a lecture, professors will give you signals to help you follow this organization. They will use specific words and expressions when they move from one idea to another. This is called *making a transition*. A transition tells you that a new idea is coming. A speaker may use a transition when he or she has finished one idea and is beginning another idea.

Listen for transitions—the words and expressions that help you follow the flow of ideas in a lecture.

**Expressions That Signal a New Idea**
- Let me start with . . .
- Now . . .
- Now, let's look at . . .
- Next, let's talk about . . .

**Expressions That Signal a Move from One Idea to Another**
- Let's move on to . . .
- Now that we've talked about . . . let's talk about . . .
- That's enough about . . . Let's go on to . . .

**H.** Work with a partner to think of other expressions that signal a transition. Write your examples here.

_____

_____

**I.** Read this excerpt from a lecture about celebrities. Then underline the lecture language that signals a transition.

Now, let me start with an interesting statistic: about 20 percent of people closely follow celebrities in the media. These people like to talk about celebrities with their friends, maybe with their husband or wife. Let's move on to talk about the category of people who believe they have a special relationship with a celebrity.

**J.** Listen to a short lecture about celebrities and the brain. Match the first part of each sentence with the correct second part.

___ **1.** When people see a celebrity,

**a.** seeing a celebrity many times.

___ **2.** The brain feels pleasure from

**b.** friends and family.

___ **3.** In the past, people felt pleasure from seeing

**c.** their brain feels pleasure.

**K.** Listen to the short lecture again. Write down the lecture language that signals a transition. Then listen again, and write down the idea that follows the transition.

**1.** Transition lecture language: _____

_____

New idea: _____

_____

**2.** Transition lecture language: _____

_____

New idea: _____

**3.** Transition lecture language: _____

_____

New idea: _____

_____

**L.** Study the meaning of these general academic words. Fill in the blanks with the correct words in the correct form. Compare your answers with a partner.

**according to:** in the opinion of, as said by

**kind:** category or type of person or thing

People today know a lot about celebrities in popular culture.

_____ media researchers, there are three

_____ of celebrity interest.

**NOTE-TAKING STRATEGY**

### Use Symbols Instead of Words

Most professors say about 125 words per minute during a lecture. You will not be able to write down every word they say. To save time, use symbols in place of words.

**Common Symbols You Can Use in Notes**

| | | | |
|---|---|---|---|
| = | is/are | + | and |
| ≠ | is not/are not | ↑ | increase, rise, go up |
| > | more than | ↓ | decrease, fall, go down |
| < | less than | △ | change, changing |
| # | number | % | percent |

**List more examples**

**A.** Work with a partner to think of other symbols you could use instead of words when taking notes. Write your examples here.

_____    _____

_____    _____

_____    _____

**Use symbols**

**B.** Read these sentences from a lecture on celebrities. Take notes using symbols in place of some of the words.

**1.** As I said, the number of celebrity magazines is increasing.

   # celebrity magazines ↑ _____

**2.** A small number of people feel they have a special relationship with celebrities.

_____

**3.** Our ideas about what is beautiful always change.

_____

**4.** About 33 percent of the people in the research group have celebrity sickness.

_____

**5.** Researchers spoke with more than 100 people with celebrity sickness.

_____

**C.** Before the lecture, think about everything you have learned and discussed about the media and celebrities. What do you expect to learn from the lecture? Write three predictions below. Compare your predictions with a partner.

1. _____

2. _____

3. _____

**D.** Watch the lecture, and take notes using symbols instead of words when you can. Remember to listen for the lecture language that signals a transition.

Topic:



Increase in amount of celebrity news coverage:



Reasons for increase in celebrity coverage:



Effects of increased media coverage:

**E.** Circle the answer that best describes how well you were able to
understand the lecture language.

I was able to recognize when the professor moved from one idea
to another ___.

**a.** all of the time  **b.** most of the time  **c.** sometimes  **d.** not often

**F.** Use your notes to answer these questions.

**1.** What has happened to news coverage in the last 35 years? Why?

_____

_____

_____

**2.** What are two reasons for the increase in the amount of celebrity
coverage?

_____

_____

_____

**3.** What are two negative results of the increase in celebrity coverage?

_____

_____

_____

_____

**G.** Were you able to answer the questions in Exercise F using the
information in your notes? Compare and discuss your notes with a few
other students. Help each other fill in any missing information. Revise
your notes.

**H.** Work with a partner. Review your notes from the lecture. Then
summarize the main points of the lecture for your partner. Take turns,
and talk for 2-3 minutes only.

**ACADEMIC
DISCUSSION
STRATEGY**

### Interrupt and Ask for Clarification

During class discussions, students do not always understand everything the professor or their classmates say. This is normal. When this happens to you, you may need to ask people to repeat or explain their ideas. During a discussion, politely interrupt and ask questions when you don't understand something.

**Actions to Let Others Know You Want to Interrupt**
- Make eye contact with the person who is speaking.
- Make a small hand gesture.
- Raise your hand.

**Expressions to Use for Interrupting**
- Excuse me, . . .
- I'm sorry, . . .
- Before we go on, . . .

**Questions to Ask When You Don't Understand**
- Could you repeat that, please?
- Could you say that again, please?
- Could you explain that?
- What does that mean?

List more examples

**A.** Work with a partner to think of other expressions for interrupting and asking for clarification. Write your examples here.

_____

_____

_____

**B.** In a group, read and discuss the questions. Keep the conversation going until every student has had a chance to practice interrupting and asking for clarification. Use your own ideas or the ones given below.

1. What's the best way to learn about celebrities?

   **Possible Ideas**
   look at celebrity Web sites
   watch a celebrity television show

2. Tell each other about a time when you or a friend saw a real celebrity. What happened? How did you feel?

**C.** Discuss these ideas with your classmates. Remember to use the expressions for interrupting and asking for clarification.

1. How big of a problem is the increase in celebrity media coverage?

2. Do you think there will be even more celebrity coverage in the future? If so, what kind of coverage will it be? What might cause the amount of celebrity coverage to decrease?

3. The professor explained two of the negative effects of celebrity media news. What are some possible positive effects of celebrity coverage?

4. Look back at your notes. What was another idea in the lecture that you found important or interesting? Tell the class why you think it is important or interesting. Ask for your classmates' opinions.

**STEP 4** Present Your Knowledge

**PRESENTATION STRATEGY**

**Create Rapport with the Audience**

It is important for a speaker to create rapport—that is, a friendly relationship—with the audience. When a speaker makes a connection with the audience, the audience feels more comfortable. They are more likely to pay attention. A speaker can create rapport by using effective eye contact and by smiling. There are also several expressions a speaker can use to create a friendly relationship with the audience.

Create rapport with your audience to help them feel comfortable with you.

**Check your comprehension**

**A.** Watch a student give a presentation about a celebrity. Answer these two questions.

**1.** Who is the celebrity?

_____

**2.** What is the speaker's opinion about the amount of coverage the celebrity gets?

_____

**Notice rapport**

**GO ONLINE**

**B.** Watch the video again. Think about the information in the strategy box above. List two problems with the student's rapport with the audience.

_____

_____

**GO ONLINE** **C.** The student received some suggestions about her presentation and delivered it again. Watch the new presentation. In your notebook, list two improvements the student made to create rapport with the audience.

**PRESENTATION STRATEGY**

**Strategies for Creating Rapport with Your Audience**

Smile and make eye contact with the audience.

Point out that you have something in common with the audience, such as an experience, habit, or attitude. Use expressions like these:

- All of us have seen . . .
- If you're like me, you . . .
- We all like to . . .

**List more examples**

**D.** Work with a partner to think of other ways to create rapport with an audience. Write your examples here.

_____

_____

**Practice creating rapport**

**E.** Work in a group. Have each student choose one of the questions below. Think about your answer. Then stand in front of your group, and answer the question. Use the strategies for creating rapport with your audience.

**1.** Do you think celebrities are paid too much? Why or why not?

**2.** What's the difference between a famous person and a celebrity? Give some examples.

**3.** Which celebrities would you invite to dinner? Why?

**4.** Do you think celebrities like being celebrities? Why or why not?

**5.** Would you like to be a celebrity? Why or why not?

After you finish, have your classmates give you feedback on your rapport. Ask them these two questions:

**1.** What are two ways I effectively created rapport?

**2.** What is one way to improve how I create rapport?

**Give a presentation**

**F.** Develop and deliver a presentation about celebrity coverage in the media.

Choose a celebrity in music, sports, or movies and television. For one week, follow news about the celebrity. Use the Internet, television, magazines, or newspapers. Notice how many stories are reported about the person. Present what you noticed to your class. Give your opinion about whether the amount of coverage this celebrity gets is appropriate. Use the strategies for creating rapport with your audience.

Before you prepare your presentation, review the ideas and vocabulary from this chapter.

**Think about the topic**

**A.** Look at the pictures of four ways to store information. Then work with a partner to answer the questions below.

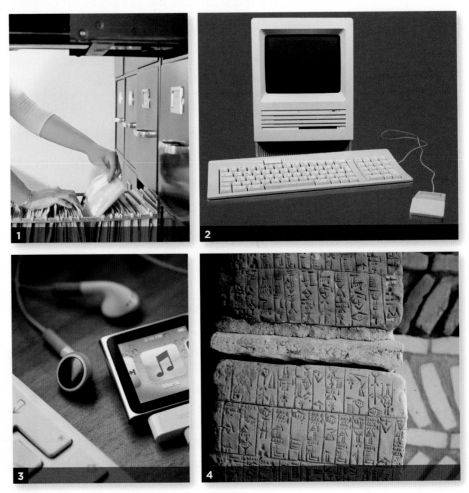

1. Which of the four storage methods takes up the most space? Which one takes up the least space?

2. Which storage method holds the most information? Which one holds the least information?

3. What do you predict will change in the future of information technology?

4. What inventions or new behaviors will we see in the next 20 years?

**B.** Read this section from a history textbook about early written communication.

## A Look at the Beginnings of Mass Communication

A writing system is one of the most important inventions of humankind, just behind the wheel and the ability to use fire. Historians say that the invention of a writing system was the beginning of mass communication. The earliest full writing system is more than 5,000 years old. It comes from the Middle East in what was then called Sumeria. The Sumerians had a story to explain their invention of writing:

*The king of Uruk sent one of his servants to another kingdom far away with an important message. The messenger arrived at the court so exhausted from the journey that he was not able to **convey** his message orally—he was too tired to speak. The king heard about this and was upset. He developed a clever solution. From then on, when he wanted to send a message, he made a flat **tablet** out of wet clay. He cut the message into the soft clay. The tablet was the **medium** for the message. There was no alphabet or writing system, so he used pictures to write the message. Each picture or symbol was equal to a word or idea.*

Though this story is interesting, it should be ***taken with a grain of salt***: it is likely more myth than fact. Historians ask, why would the king write a letter if the **receiver** could not read it? They also doubt that the earliest writing system was a written version of speech. It is more likely that writing began as a separate system of communication. It was probably developed to keep track of weighing and measuring animals and foods.

Historians agree on a few things, however. Early writing was *pictographic*—based on pictures, not sounds—and messages were carved into heavy clay tablets. Most importantly, they agree that writing systems were invented to **store** and **transmit** information. Prior to writing, communication was strictly "face to face"; people only knew what others told them in person. Important information was not **accessible** to all people. With the invention of a writing system, information became **portable**. Writing allowed people to share their words and knowledge with others, near and far away.

**Check your comprehension**

**C.** With a partner, discuss these questions about the reading.

1. What were the two main reasons that a writing system was invented?

2. What is a pictographic system of writing?

3. What does it mean for information to be portable?

**D.** Circle the answer that correctly completes the definition of the underlined word. Look back at the reading on page 67 to check your answers.

1. To <u>convey</u> a message or information means that you _____ it.

   **a.** change　　　　　　**b.** communicate

2. A <u>tablet</u> is a flat piece of ____ that people in the past cut words into.

   **a.** clay or stone　　　**b.** thick paper

3. Television is an example of a <u>medium</u>. It is one way that _____ can move from place to place.

   **a.** messengers　　　　**b.** information

4. The <u>receiver</u> of a message refers to the person who _____.

   **a.** gets it　　　　　　**b.** sends it

5. When you <u>store</u> information on a computer, you _____ the information there.

   **a.** create or make　　**b.** keep or hold

6. When you <u>transmit</u> information, you _____ places and people.

   **a.** keep it away from　**b.** send or pass it between

7. For information to be <u>accessible</u>, people have to be able to use it or get it _____.

   **a.** easily　　　　　　**b.** privately

8. <u>Portable</u> information is information that people can easily _____.

   **a.** change or correct　**b.** carry or move

**E.** Circle the phrase with a similar meaning to the underlined idiom.

That writer is famous for telling wild stories about himself. The article he wrote about his childhood should be <u>taken with a grain of salt</u>.

**a.** believed as fact　**b.** not completely believed　**c.** never believed

**F.** Discuss these questions in a group. Share your answers with the class.

1. How would the world be different if writing were never invented? Use your imagination and think of some examples of life without writing.

2. What are some of the ways that transmitting information has changed during your lifetime?

**G.** To help you understand the listening strategy, discuss the situation below with a partner. Then answer the questions.

During a lecture, you sit next to a student who is listening and taking notes. When the professor uses an unfamiliar word, the student stops taking notes and looks up the new word in a dictionary. Is this a good strategy to use during a lecture? Why or why not?

---

**LISTENING STRATEGY**

**Recognize Lecture Language That Signals a Definition**

Professors often use new words as they explain information. They also use a variety of expressions to signal a definition for those words.

Listen for the words and expressions that professors use to signal a definition.

**Expressions That Signal a Definition**

- That is, . . .
- In other words, . . .
- X, meaning . . .
- By X, I mean . . .
- Let me define that: . . .
- The definition of that is . . .

---

**H.** Work with a partner to think of other expressions that signal a definition. Write your examples here.

_____

_____

_____

---

**I.** Read this excerpt from a lecture on writing tools. Then do the following:

- Circle the word or phrase that the professor wants to define.
- Underline the lecture language that signals the definition.
- Put a box around the definition.

Now that we know a little bit about the invention of writing, let's look at the tools that early writers wrote with. When people were writing on clay tablets, they were using bone tools. As the medium moved from clay to early paper, people began to use reed brushes and pens. Now, by reeds, I mean grasses that usually grow by a river. These were writing tools. When pens were first invented, they were made out of quills,... quills, meaning the end of a bird feather. But by 1850, quill pens were less common because the quality of steel nibs, . . . let me define that: the metal points of pens were called steel nibs, . . . these nibs were now very good quality and replaced quills.

**J.** Listen to a short lecture about recent communication tools. Match the first part of each sentence with the correct second part.

___ **1.** Recent communication has been influenced by

    **a.** send information to large audiences.

___ **2.** Television and radio have made it easier to

    **b.** without wires.

___ **3.** Radio sends out signals

    **c.** technology.

**K.** Listen to the short lecture again. Write down the lecture language that signals a definition. Then listen again, and write down the definition.

**1.** Word: technology

Lecture language: _____

Definition: _____

_____

**2.** Word: television

Lecture language: _____

Definition: _____

_____

**3.** Word: radio

Lecture language: _____

Definition: _____

_____

**L.** Study the meaning of these general academic words. Fill in the blanks with the correct words in the correct form. Compare your answers with a partner.

**major:** very important, especially when compared to other things of a similar kind

**focus on:** to give special attention to a subject

In today's lecture, I want to _____ how technology has affected communication. Then, we'll discuss one _____ invention in particular—the telephone.

**NOTE-TAKING STRATEGY**

## Use Abbreviations Instead of Full Words

In Chapter 5, you learned how to use symbols to represent some words and help you take notes more quickly. You can also use a short form, or abbreviation, of some common words. Use abbreviations instead of full words to help you write down ideas more quickly.

### Commonly Used Abbreviations

| | | | | | | |
|---|---|---|---|---|---|---|
| avg | average | est | estimate | info | information |
| approx | approximately | esp | especially | max | maximum |
| btwn | between | etc. | et cetera (and other similar things) | min | minimum |
| cont | continued | | | vs | versus |
| diff | difference | id | identify | w/ | with |
| ea | each | i.e. | in other words | w/out | without |
| e.g. | example | imp | important | yr | year |

**List more examples**

**A.** Work with a partner to think of other abbreviations. Write your examples here.

_____

_____

**Ue abbreviations**

**B.** Read these sentences from a lecture on the invention of writing. Take notes in your notebook using abbreviations in place of some of the words and ideas. Compare your notes with a partner.

**1.** The first writing system was developed approximately 5,200 years ago. It was pictographic writing invented by the Sumerians.

1st writing system developed approx 5,200 yrs ago

pictographic writing—Sumerians

**2.** The writing that the Sumerians invented is called *cuneiform*. Cuneiform writing is wedge-shaped, like a piece of cake.

**3.** The information was written down using symbols that were shaped liked wedges.

**4.** There are some differences between types of early picture-based writing. For example, if we look at cuneiform writing versus Egyptian hieroglyphics, we see that cuneiform is more abstract—in other words, it is more like shapes—and hieroglyphics are more like pictures.

**C.** Before the lecture, think about everything you have learned and discussed about communication. What do you expect to learn from the lecture? Write three predictions below. Compare your predictions with a partner.

1. _____

2. _____

3. _____

**D.** Watch the lecture, and take notes using abbreviations. Remember to listen for the lecture language that signals a definition.

Topic:

Mass communication:

Communication revolutions:

Ideas key to mass communication:

**E.** Circle the answer that best describes how well you were able to
understand the lecture language.

I was able to recognize when the professor gave a definition _____.

**a.** all of the time    **b.** most of the time    **c.** sometimes    **d.** not often

**F.** Use your notes to answer these questions.

**1.** What is the definition of mass communication?

_____

_____

_____

**2.** What two problems about early written communication were discussed?

_____

_____

_____

**3.** What are the three communication revolutions discussed in the lecture?

_____

_____

_____

_____

**4.** What three ideas are key to mass communication?

_____

_____

_____

_____

**G.** Were you able to answer the questions in Exercise F using the
information in your notes? Compare and discuss your notes with a few
other students. Help each other fill in any missing information. Revise
your notes.

**H.** Work with a partner. Review your notes from the lecture. Then
summarize the main points of the lecture for your partner. Take turns,
and talk for 2-3 minutes only.

**ACADEMIC DISCUSSION STRATEGY**

**Ask for More Information**

During a discussion, you might be interested in an idea and want to understand it better, or you might need to know more about it for a test or assignment. In a discussion, politely ask questions to get more information about a point or idea.

**Expressions for Asking for More Information**
- Could you explain more about . . .?
- What is an example of that?
- How does that work?
- What do you mean by that?
- What's the difference between . . . and . . . ?

List more examples

**A.** Work with a partner to think of other expressions for asking for more information. Write your example here.

_____

_____

_____

_____

**Practice asking for more information**

**B.** In a group, read and discuss the questions. Keep the conversation going until every student has had a chance to practice asking for more information. Use your own ideas or the ones given below.

1. What are some of the ways that people use written language to communicate ideas? Is this changing? Why or why not?

   **Possible Ideas**
   They write letters to friends.
   They write papers for school.
   They write notes to roommates.

2. What are some of the ways that you use computer technology to communicate with others and to learn about ideas? Discuss some specific examples.

   **Possible Ideas**
   email
   research
   instant messages

**Discuss the ideas in the lecture**

**C.** Discuss these ideas with your classmates. Remember to use the expressions for asking for more information.

1. Over the centuries, wider communication has become possible between people in many different societies. What are some of the results of this worldwide exchange of ideas and information?

2. Knowledge and information are no longer in the hands of only a few privileged people. Do you think this is a good thing? Why or why not?

3. The lecture states that there are three ideas key to mass communication. Review these ideas. Can you predict what a future communication revolution might be?

4. Look back at your notes. What was another idea in the lecture that you found important or interesting? Tell the class why you think it is important or interesting. Ask for your classmates' opinions.

**PRESENTATION STRATEGY**

### Open the Floor to Questions

It's important for the speaker to let the audience know when the presentation is finished. The speaker can do this by first thanking the audience. At this point the audience might not have understood everything the speaker said. Therefore, it's helpful to invite the audience to ask questions about the ideas in the presentation. Inviting the audience to ask questions is called *opening the floor*.

Open the floor to questions at the end of your presentation to be sure your audience has understood all of your ideas.

**Check your comprehension**

**GO ONLINE**

**A.** Watch a student give the end of a presentation about his use of mass media. Answer these two questions.

**1.** What two types of media does the student compare?

_____

**2.** What device does the student prefer for getting information?

_____

**Notice how the speaker opens the floor to questions**

**GO ONLINE**

**B.** Watch the video again. Think about the information in the strategy box above. List two problems with the way the student opens the floor to questions.

_____

_____

**GO ONLINE**  **C.** The student received some suggestions on his presentation and delivered it again. Watch the new presentation. List two improvements the student made to the way he finished the presentation.

_____

_____

_____

**PRESENTATION STRATEGY**

**Expressions for Opening the Floor to Questions**
• Thank you. Do you have any questions?
• Thank you for your interest. I'm happy to answer questions.
• Thank you for listening. Now I'd like to take your questions.

**List more examples** **D.** Work with a partner to think of other expressions for opening the floor to questions. Write your examples here.

_____

_____

_____

**Practice opening the floor** **E.** Stand in front of a group of classmates. Tell your group about the mass communication devices you use. Explain the information you receive on them. When you finish, thank your audience. Then open the floor to questions.

**Note:** Make sure you understand each question before answering it. To do this, use language for asking for clarification from page 62.

After you finish, have your classmates give you feedback on how you opened the floor to questions. Ask them these two questions:

**1.** What are two ways I effectively opened the floor to questions?

**2.** What is one way to improve how I open the floor to questions?

**Give a presentation** **F.** Develop and deliver a presentation comparing two types of mass media that you use.

Choose two types of mass media:
• Audio: radio, podcasts
• Print: newspapers, books, magazines
• Visual: television, film
• Digital: computers, the Internet

Describe the kind of information you get through each type of mass media. Compare the two types of media. Give your opinion about which type of media you prefer and why. When you finish, use the strategy for opening the floor to questions.

Before you prepare your presentation, review the ideas and vocabulary from this chapter.

**A.** Work in a group. Analyze celebrity coverage in a magazine or newspaper.

Choose an English-language news magazine or newspaper. Look at the most recent issue. Together, find and count the number of articles about celebrities.

### Discuss the Coverage
Discuss these questions in your group:

• Are you surprised by the number of articles about celebrities?

• Would you guess that there are more of these articles now than there were one year ago? Five years ago? Ten years ago? Why or why not?

• Has this activity changed your opinion of the magazine or newspaper? Why or why not?

### Present What You Find
Present your results to the class. Open the floor to questions, and be prepared to answer them.

**B.** Work in a group. Follow the steps to create a survey about mass media and communications.

Work with others in your group to develop a survey about communications and mass media today. You may also ask people's predictions for the next communication revolution. Create four or five questions that you feel will draw the information you want from people.

### Listen and Take Notes
Individually survey five people of different ages. Ask them the questions your group creates, and take careful notes of their answers.

### Discuss the Results
Discuss the results with your group, and record the results in a chart. Draw two or three general conclusions about your results.

### Present Your Conclusions
Present your group's results to the class. Be careful to maintain a good rapport with your audience.

# Unit Goals

## CHAPTER 7
**Learn how sleep affects thinking**

**Listening Strategy**
• Recognize lecture language that signals an example

**Note-Taking Strategy**
• Organize lecture material into visual form

**Academic Discussion Strategy**
• Express agreement and disagreement in the discussion

**Presentation Strategy**
• Support your presentation with effective word visuals

## CHAPTER 8
**Learn how geography influences culture**

**Listening Strategy**
• Recognize lecture language that signals an explanation

**Note-Taking Strategy**
• Organize ideas into a chart

**Academic Discussion Strategy**
• Show respect for others' opinions during the discussion

**Presentation Strategy**
• Speak effectively about visuals during a presentation

# UNIT
# 4

# Science

science \ˈsaɪəns\ The study of the physical world and natural laws

**Think about the topic**  **A.** Take this quiz about your sleep habits. Then work with a partner to answer the questions below.

## Your Sleep Habits

**1.** Most nights, I sleep _____.
  **a.** fewer than 6 hours
  **b.** 6-8 hours
  **c.** 9 or more hours

**2.** I am most likely to skip sleep in order to _____.
  **a.** study
  **b.** work
  **c.** watch TV
  **d.** hang out with friends
  **e.** I don't skip sleep.

**3.** I usually make up for lost sleep by _____.
  **a.** taking naps during the day
  **b.** sleeping late on the weekends
  **c.** adjusting my schedule
  **d.** adapting to less sleep

**1.** Are your answers similar to or different from your partner's answers?

**2.** Which of your answers do you think is the most interesting?

**3.** Which of your partner's answers is the most interesting? Why?

**4.** Do you think it is possible to make up for lost sleep? Why or why not?

**B.** Read this brochure about how lack of sleep can affect academic performance.

# The Importance of Sleep to Academic Success

It's no secret that many college students do not sleep enough. Academic studies, social life, part-time or full-time jobs, and relationships are often more important than sleep. Students experience even more sleep **deprivation** as midterm and final exams approach.

## Sleep Is Serious Business

Lack of sleep can cause these harmful **side effects:**

- daytime **drowsiness**
- inability to **cope with** stress
- weight gain
- poor health
- low energy

Most importantly for students, sleep deprivation makes studying and learning more difficult. It also hurts the body's ability to stay healthy.

A recent poll shows that many young adults are suffering from sleep deprivation that is severe enough to **impair** daytime activities. These young people get an average of 6.8 hours of rest per night, but many **function** on much less. According to current research, most undergraduates need 8.5 to 9.25 hours of sleep (most adults, 7 to 9 hours).

## Burning the Candle at Both Ends

College life only increases the problem of sleep deprivation because students try to **burn the candle at both ends**. Some students work a part-time job to help pay for college expenses. Some students have to support a family while going to school. Stress from these pressures can lead to insomnia—the inability to sleep.

Sleeplessness is especially bad as final exams approach and students **cram** for exams. When students force themselves to stay awake to study, they have to function on even less sleep. Too many nights of staying awake can lead to **long-term** sleep problems.

## Sleep Is a Necessity, Not a Luxury

Your top academic performance depends on getting enough sleep. So remember, as you plan your schedule, be sure to allow plenty of time for sleep. You will have more energy, better health, and greater chances for academic success!

---

**Check your comprehension**

**C.** With a partner, discuss these questions about the reading.

1. What are three negative results of not getting enough sleep? *low energy poor health weight gain*

2. How much sleep do college students need, and how much do they usually get? *students need 8.5 to 9.25 hours of sleep students usually gets an average of 6.8 hours of sleep*

3. What is the approximate amount of sleep college students lose per night? *3 to 4 hours*

4. What are two reasons that college students don't get enough sleep? *most students work part time jobs and the stress from work would lead to less sleep.*

**D.** Match the words from the reading with their definitions. Look back at
the reading on page 81 to check your answers.

_b_ **1.** deprivation    **a.** the feeling of being tired and almost asleep

_d_ **2.** side effect    **b.** lack of something considered to be a necessity

_a_ **3.** drowsiness    **c.** to work in the correct way

_h_ **4.** cope with    **d.** a negative secondary result of something

_f_ **5.** impair    **e.** to prepare yourself for a test by studying a lot
of information quickly

_c_ **6.** function    **f.** to damage something or to make it worse

_e_ **7.** cram    **g.** lasting into the future

_g_ **8.** long-term    **h.** to deal successfully with a difficult situation

**E.** Circle the phrase with a similar meaning to the underlined idiom.

It is possible to <u>burn the candle at both ends</u> for a short amount of time,
but after a while you have to slow down and take a break. If you don't,
your performance will become worse.

**a.** do boring things    **b.** do a few things    **(c.)** do many things at once

**F.** Discuss these questions in a group. Share your answers with the class.

1. Have you ever felt as if you were burning the candle at both ends?
What was the situation? What finally happened?

2. How do you stay awake when you need to study? Have you ever
experienced any of the side effects of sleep deprivation mentioned in
the brochure? What happened?

**G.** With a partner, discuss three things that you have learned from the
reading and from your discussion about the importance of sleep.

1. _____

_____

2. _____

_____

3. _____

_____

**H.** To help you understand the listening strategy, discuss the situation below with a partner. Then answer the question.

Imagine someone asks you, "What does *burning the candle at both ends* mean?"

Without using a dictionary, how can you explain the meaning quickly and easily?

**LISTENING
STRATEGY**

### Recognize Lecture Language That Signals an Example

Professors usually give many examples during a lecture. These examples help students understand general ideas.

Listen for the words and expressions that professors use to signal an example.

**Expressions That Signal an Example**
- For example, . . .
- Here are some examples: . . .
- Take X, for example.
- For instance, . . .
- . . . , such as . . .
- Let me give you an example.

**List more examples**

**I.** Work with a partner to think of other expressions that signal an example. Write your examples here.

_____

_____

_____

**Recognize example
lecture language**

**J.** Read this excerpt from a lecture on the effects of sleep deprivation. Then do the following:

- Circle the lecture language that signals an example.
- Underline the example.

Lack of sleep causes many problems. (For example,) it hurts the body's ability to stay healthy. Usually, this is the result of the fact that the immune system—the part of the body that protects us from infection—is weakened without sleep. (Let me give you an example) of what happens. It is easier to get infections, (such as) colds and flu. Another problem that occurs is weight gain. This happens because the body loses the ability to handle sugar; (for instance,) it turns sugar into fat rather than burning it as energy.

*the mean idea: Problems caused by luck of ssleep*

**K.** Listen to a short lecture about driving while drowsy. Match the first part of each sentence with the correct second part.

___ **1.** It's a problem to feel drowsy when driving because

___ **2.** It's good to pull over and take a nap because

___ **3.** It is not a good idea to listen to loud music because

**a.** the effect doesn't work for very long.

**b.** drivers can't concentrate and react quickly.

**c.** you feel less tired after resting.

**L.** Listen to the short lecture again. Write down the lecture language that signals an example. Then listen again, and write down the examples.

**1.** Idea: loud noise

Example lecture language: _____

Example: _____

_____

**2.** Idea: caffeine

Example lecture language: _____

Example: _____

_____

**3.** Idea: sleep

Example lecture language: _____

Example: _____

_____

**M.** Study the meaning of these general academic words. Fill in the blanks with the correct words in the correct form. Compare your answers with a partner.

**evidence:** one or more reasons (e.g., facts, objects, or signs) for believing that something is or is not true

**area:** a particular subject or range of interest

This team of researchers has studied sleep for many years. They concentrate on the _____ of sleep deprivation. I'm going to present some of the _____ from their studies to show you the serious nature of the issue.

**NOTE-TAKING STRATEGY**

### Use a Visual Form

Sometimes, it is easier to remember the ideas in a lecture when you record them as a picture. Using a visual form of the ideas in the lecture helps you see how the ideas are connected. Record information in a visual form to remind yourself of how the ideas in the lecture relate to each other.

The following is an excerpt from a lecture and one student's notes.

Today I'd like to discuss some of the advice that is given on how to improve sleep. I'll talk about three major areas to consider. These are psychological solutions, meaning what can we do to get our minds to relax. Physical solutions, meaning what we can do to get our bodies to relax. And finally, the things we can do to improve our sleep environment, that is, the space that we sleep in.

**Analyze the notes**

**A.** Look at the excerpt and notes above. With a partner, discuss these questions.

**1.** How did the student indicate the topic of this section of the lecture?

**2.** How did the student indicate the three areas to consider?

**3.** How does the student indicate examples?

**Take notes using a visual form**

**B.** Read this excerpt from a lecture on advice about sleep disorders. Take notes in your notebook. Use a visual form.

Today we'll talk about sleep disorders. There are two major categories of sleep disorders. I'll start by explaining insomnia. Insomnia is the word used for difficulty in falling asleep or remaining asleep. About 35 percent of adults in the United States experience insomnia. The second category of sleep disorders makes it difficult for people to stay awake. People with these disorders are very sleepy during normal waking hours, even though they sleep normally at night. This condition is less common than insomnia. Only about 5 percent to 10 percent of people have it.

Make predictions

See page 8

**C.** Before the lecture, think about everything you have learned and discussed about the topic of sleep. What do you expect to learn from the lecture? Write three predictions below. Compare your predictions with a partner.

1. _____

2. _____

3. _____

Watch the lecture

GO ONLINE

**D.** Watch the lecture, and take notes. Use a visual form when appropriate. Remember to listen for the lecture language that signals an example.

Topic:

Need for sleep:

Effects of sleep deprivation:

The frontal lobe:

**E.** Circle the answer that best describes how well you were able to
understand the lecture language.

I was able to recognize when the professor gave examples _____.

**a.** all of the time    **b.** most of the time    **c.** sometimes    **d.** not often

**F.** Use your notes to answer these questions.

1. What are two of the reasons that people need sleep?

_____

_____

2. Why is sleep especially important for students?

_____

_____

_____

_____

3. How are human bodies affected by sleep deprivation?

_____

_____

_____

_____

4. How do people act when sleep deprivation affects the frontal lobe of
the brain?

_____

_____

_____

_____

**G.** Were you able to answer the questions in Exercise F using the
information in your notes? Compare and discuss your notes with a few
other students. Help each other fill in any missing information. Revise
your notes.

**H.** Work with a partner. Review your notes from the lecture. Then
summarize the main points of the lecture for your partner. Take turns,
and talk for 2–3 minutes only.

**ACADEMIC DISCUSSION STRATEGY**

### Agree and Disagree

During a group discussion, you might want to agree or disagree with another student and say more about an idea. This type of exchange is good because it shows how well you understand the topic.

Use expressions to agree or disagree with others in a discussion.

### Expressions for Agreeing

- I agree with John.
- That's a good point.
- John is right.

### Expressions for Disagreeing

- I don't agree with that.
- I disagree with John.
- I'm sorry, but I have to disagree.
- I have a different idea.

**List more examples**  **A.** Work with a partner to think of other expressions for agreeing and disagreeing with others during a discussion. Write your examples here.

_____

_____

_____

_____

**B.** Read each statement about sleep, and decide whether you think it is true or false. Then in a group, explain and defend your choice. Keep the conversation going until every student has had a chance to practice agreeing and disagreeing.

Write T for true or F for false.

____ **1.** Men need more sleep than women.

____ **2.** Not everyone dreams every night.

____ **3.** As adults get older, they need less sleep.

____ **4.** If you play audio lessons during the night, you can learn while you sleep.

____ **5.** If you have insomnia at night, you should take a long nap during the day.

**C.** Discuss these ideas with your classmates. Remember to use the expressions for agreeing and disagreeing.

**1.** Have you ever had too much sleep? What was the situation? What effect does too much sleep have on a person's mind, body, and personality?

**2.** On your own, write a list of five pieces of advice for a classmate who is having trouble sleeping. Then compare your advice with the other students in your group. Work together to create one list with only five pieces of advice on it. You must agree on these five pieces of advice and put them in order from the most effective to the least effective.

**3.** Look back at your notes. What was another idea in the lecture that you found important or interesting? Tell the class why you think it is important or interesting. Ask for your classmates' opinions.

**PRESENTATION STRATEGY**

**Make Word Visuals**

A visual is any printed item speakers use to help their audience follow their presentation. Visuals can be charts, maps, or pictures. Speakers also create visuals with words. Word visuals show the topic, lists, definitions, or questions. Speakers can display words on a poster board, an overhead projector, or electronic presentation slides. Word visuals should highlight what the speaker is saying. They should not be a copy of what the speaker says. Word visuals should keep the audience's attention and help them follow the ideas in the presentation. Word visuals should be easy for the audience to read.

Make word visuals to keep the audience's attention and to help them follow your ideas.

Notice word visuals

**A.** Look at the word visuals below. List two ways these visuals are **not** effective.

Ineffective Word Visual 1                Ineffective Word Visual 2

_____        _____

_____        _____

_____        _____

_____        _____

 **B.** The student received some suggestions on her visuals and recreated them. Watch the presentation with the new visuals. List two improvements the student made to her word visuals.

_____

_____

**Strategies for Creating Effective Word Visuals**
- Make letters big enough for everyone in the room to read.
- Leave space between lines.
- Express each idea with a phrase, not a full sentence.

**List more examples** **C.** Work with a partner to think of other ways to make effective word visuals. Write your ideas in your notebook.

**Practice making word visuals** **D.** Imagine you will present the information below. You decide to make word visuals to help your audience follow the ideas in your presentation. Make two to three word visuals using this information.

Many universities are trying to help students develop better sleep habits. For example, Duke University has made special study rooms with relaxing environments. In some cases, students sit in a massage chair and listen to a water fountain. The University of California at Los Angeles is offering a ten-week course to help students who have sleep problems. Rice University is teaching students about the importance of having a regular bedtime.

After you make your word visuals, have a group of classmates give you feedback. Ask them these two questions:

**1.** What are two ways my word visuals were effective?

**2.** What is one way to improve my word visuals?

**Give a presentation** **E.** Develop and deliver a presentation about your classmates' sleep habits.

Choose a sleep-related topic such as amount of sleep, dreams, napping, staying awake to study, or how lack of sleep affects school performance. Create survey questions to ask all of your classmates.

Make word visuals to present the survey results. Use the strategies for creating effective word visuals.

Before you prepare your presentation, review the ideas and vocabulary from this chapter.

**Think about the topic**

**A.** Look at the pictures of geographical features. Then work with a partner to answer the questions below.

1. What geographical features (desert, forest, etc.) are in these pictures?

2. What other geographical features can you think of?

3. Describe the climate and main geographical features of the area where you grew up.

4. If you could live in or near one of these places, which place would you choose? Why?

**B.** Read this article about the geographical features that helped create Silicon Valley.

# Geography Helps Explain the Success of Silicon Valley

*Silicon Valley* is a commonly used nickname for the southern part of the San Francisco Bay Area in California. Silicon **Valley** is a specific geographic area—the northern part of Santa Clara Valley and surrounding communities on the San Francisco Peninsula and in the East Bay. Its name, however, comes from the world of technology. This area has a high concentration of computer-related companies that make and use silicon chips.

How did this small area become the center of such an innovative and successful industry? Many people point to geography to explain Silicon Valley's high-tech success. Pleasant climate and available space are two geographical features that attract people and companies to Silicon Valley. These features hold them there. In a survey of Silicon Valley companies, more than two-thirds rated the **location** and climate as outstanding.

Other factors have helped Silicon Valley's success as well. Although the area exists in a valley,

it is not **isolated**. There are major universities—a key factor in the **spread** of new ideas and in training workers. It is also close to San Francisco, a major city and financial center. This means investment money is available.

Some of the biggest markets for Silicon Valley's products are Japan, Taiwan, and South Korea. Oakland is one of the few major ports on the West Coast of the United States, making it easier to **exchange** goods. These geographical advantages have helped Silicon Valley overcome some of the **barriers** to trade that exist in other regions. They encourage rather than **inhibit** business relationships.

When you consider geography, access to new technology, availability of investment money, and ease of transport, there isn't much to **prevent** Silicon Valley's growth and success. **The bottom line** is, geography has helped make Silicon Valley the heart of the high-tech industry in the United States.

**C.** With a partner, discuss these questions about the reading.

1. Where and what is Silicon Valley?

2. What three geographical features help explain the success of Silicon Valley? Vally – major ports.

3. Silicon Valley is close to an ocean and a port city on a bay. What influence do these two geographical features have on business in the area? making it easier to Exchange goods.

**D.** Circle the answer that correctly completes the definition of the
underlined word. Look back at the reading on page 93 to check
your answers.

1. A <u>valley</u> is an area of _____ land between two hills or mountains.

   **a.** drier                    **(b.)** lower

2. The <u>location</u> of something refers to its _____.

   **(a.)** place or position       **b.** geographical features

3. To be <u>isolated</u> means to be _____ other things.

   **(a.)** far away from           **b.** close to

4. When ideas <u>spread</u>, _____ people know about them.

   **a.** fewer                    **(b.)** more

5. An <u>exchange</u> occurs when one person or company gives something to
   another, and the other person or company gives _____.

   **(a.)** something in return     **b.** thanks

6. <u>Barriers</u> are things that _____ two areas or groups of people.

   **a.** bring together           **(b.)** separate

7. To <u>inhibit</u> something is to keep it from _____ in the usual or
   expected way.

   **a.** going away               **(b.)** continuing

8. When you <u>prevent</u> something, you _____ happen.

   **a.** help it                  **(b.)** don't let it

**E.** Circle the phrase with a similar meaning to the underlined idiom.

Some people don't like Silicon Valley, but <u>the bottom line</u> is, if you work
in the computer industry, you will probably have to spend time there.

   **a.** the traditional way    **b.** the best system    **(c.)** the core idea

**F.** Discuss these questions in a group. Share your answers with the class.

1. Think about the main geographical features of the city that you live in or
   grew up in. What influences do they have on the area?

2. What geographical features might have a negative influence on the
   success of an area? Why?

*[Handwritten notes:]*
F)-1) the main geographical Feature in the Allentown is a vally has water. east area up, the mountnin Protect the huracns

*[near F.1:]* allentown vally

*[after F.2:]* No, it very hote on morning and very coold on night

**G.** To help you understand the listening strategy, discuss the situation below with a partner. Then answer the question.

Imagine that you are going to hear a lecture on how waterways—rivers, oceans, canals—affect the development of an area. Which aspect of the lecture will help the class best understand how waterways affect development? Why? (Choose one.)

_____ **a.** an example of a waterway that has influenced development

_____ **b.** an explanation of how a waterway influences development

_____ **c.** a detailed definition of a waterway

**LISTENING
STRATEGY**

**Recognize Lecture Language That Signals an Explanation**

Professors usually give many explanations during their lectures. They describe complex processes and ideas in ways that make them easier to understand.

Listen for the words and expressions that professors use to signal an explanation.

**Expressions That Signal an Explanation**
- Let me explain . . .
- Let me show you what I mean.
- What I mean is . . .
- Let's look at how this works.

**H.** Work with a partner to think of other expressions that signal an explanation. Write your examples here.

_____

_____

**I.** Read this excerpt from a lecture on how geography affects the development of cities. Then do the following:

- Circle the lecture language that signals an explanation.
- Underline the explanation.

Today, we are going to discuss one geographical feature that has been important to the development of cities. We'll look specifically at waterways. Let me explain what I mean by waterways. By waterways, I mean rivers, lakes, ocean bays—water that is deep and wide enough for ships to travel on, to transport . . . move products back and forth. So, let me show you why waterways have been so important. In the time before railroads, and before road systems, waterways were the main way, and the least expensive way, to exchange products. So you can see that, when a city was close to a waterway, it could have more exchange of products, and as a result, more economic development.

**J.** Listen to a short lecture about the effect of waterways on culture. Match the first part of each sentence with the correct second part.

___ **1.** Waterways allow exchange of

**a.** slow development.

___ **2.** In the past, people learned about the world through

**b.** contact with other people.

___ **3.** Isolation from waterways meant

**c.** products and ideas.

**K.** Listen to the short lecture again. Write down the lecture language that signals an explanation. Then listen again, and write down the explanation.

**1.** Idea: There are many ways that we learn about the world.

Explanation lecture language:_____

Explanation: _____

_____

**2.** Idea: Waterways increased contact with other people.

Explanation lecture language:_____

Explanation: _____

_____

**3.** Idea: Cultures that live in isolation from waterways are similar.

Explanation lecture language:_____

Explanation: _____

_____

**L.** Study the meaning of these general academic words. Fill in the blanks with the correct words in the correct form. Compare your answers with a partner.

**classic example:** something that is the best or most common example of its kind

**end up:** to be or to have finally

Today, I'll discuss the geographical features that cause a city to fail. How does a city _____ with so many problems that it dies? To explain this, I'll give you a _____ of a failed city to help you understand.

### Organize Ideas into a Chart

Sometimes professors explain similarities and differences among ideas. When you know that the professor is going to present information this way, it may be easier to record the ideas in the form of a chart as you write your notes. This structure can help you remember the comparisons that the professor made. Also, notes written this way are easier to scan over. So, when you return to them before an exam, you will find them easier to read through.

The following is an excerpt from a lecture comparing waterways in Western Europe to waterways in Africa. Below it is one student's notes.

Today, I'd like to discuss how two different areas of the world, . . . two continents, . . . Europe and Africa, . . . have developed differently—and how waterways have played a role in this development. Let me start by explaining the physical features and climates of these two areas and how they vary from each other. First, physical features. Rivers in Western Europe flow gently through large, flat areas of land. They connect wide geographical areas. In Africa, rivers don't flow through flat land. In fact, they fall a thousand feet or more on their way to the sea. There are also many waterfalls that make it difficult for ships to pass. Their climates vary also. In Western Europe, rivers stay about the same all year because of regular rainfall and melting snow. But Africa's rainfall is not consistent. Rivers rise and fall dramatically with the seasons.

| Rivers | | |
|---|---|---|
| | Western Europe | Africa |
| Physical features | gentle flow over flat land | rivers fall > 1,000 ft. |
| | | result: hard for ships |
| | result: easy for ships | |
| Climate | regular rainfall/snow | no regular rainfall |
| | result: rivers regular | result: rivers vary w/ season |

**A.** Look at the excerpt and notes on page 97. With a partner, discuss these questions.

1. What main geographical feature did the student compare in the chart? How did the student indicate this?

2. How did the student indicate which two aspects are compared?

3. Where did the student put the details describing the physical features and climate of the two areas?

**B.** Before the lecture, think about everything you have learned and discussed about cultural geography. What do you expect to learn from the lecture? Write three predictions below. Compare your predictions with a partner.

1. _____

2. _____

3. _____

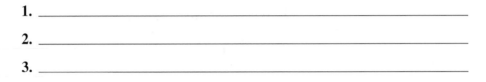

**C.** Watch the lecture, and take notes in your notebook. Use a chart when appropriate. Remember to listen for the lecture language that signals an explanation.

**D.** Circle the answer that best describes how well you were able to understand the lecture language.

I was able to recognize when the professor gave explanations ___.

**a.** all of the time          **c.** sometimes

**b.** most of the time          **d.** not often

**E.** Use your notes to answer these questions.

**1.** What is cultural geography?

_____

_____

**2.** What does *barrier effects* refer to?

_____

_____

_____

**3.** How does isolation cause differences in cultures?

_____

_____

_____

_____

**4.** Describe the physical barriers that isolate people.

_____

_____

_____

_____

**F.** Were you able to answer the questions in Exercise E using the information in your notes? Compare and discuss your notes with a few other students. Help each other fill in any missing information. Revise your notes.

**G.** Work with a partner. Review your notes from the lecture. Then summarize the main points of the lecture for your partner. Take turns, and talk for 2–3 minutes only.

**ACADEMIC DISCUSSION STRATEGY**

### Show Respect for Others' Opinions

Students often discuss different opinions in the classroom. This shows that they are thinking carefully about the topic. During a discussion, it's important to show respect for the opinions of others, especially when disagreeing. You can show respect for others by letting them know you have understood their opinion. When you show respect for others, everyone is more likely to stay involved in the discussion.

### Expressions That Show Respect for Others' Opinions
- I see your point, but . . .
- I think you are right about . . . , but I don't agree with you about . . .
- That may be true, but . . .

**List more examples**  **A.** Work with a partner to think of other expressions for showing respect for others' opinions. Write your examples here.

_____

_____

_____

_____

**B.** In a group, do the following activity. Keep the conversation going until every student has had a chance to practice showing respect for others' opinions.

Read this list of the six things that affect a culture. On your own, put them in order of the strongest (1) to the weakest (6) influence. Then compare your list with the other students in your group. Your group must create one list and agree on the order. Be prepared to explain and defend your list.

____ **Geography:** the physical features of a place

____ **Religion:** the beliefs and opinions about a higher power

____ **Language:** communication among the people of the community

____ **Media:** sources of communication such as newspapers, the Internet, television, and radio

____ **Family:** human relationships formed through genetics, adoption, or marriage

____ **Climate:** the weather

**C.** Discuss these ideas with your classmates. Remember to use the expressions for showing respect for others' opinions.

1. Imagine that you live in a country surrounded by physical barriers. How do you think the barriers would affect the culture? Would isolation bring people closer together? Would people become more tolerant of each other, or would the rules become more strict?

2. In the modern world, geography is less of a barrier between cultures. In which ways is this good for a culture? In which ways is this bad?

3. Explain why you agree or disagree with the following statement: Geography creates limits, but people determine what they will do within those limits.

4. Look back at your notes. What was another idea in the lecture that you found important or interesting? Tell the class why you think it is important or interesting. Ask for your classmates' opinions.

**PRESENTATION STRATEGY**

**Speak Effectively about Visuals**

A visual with an image such as an illustration, photo, or map, can help the audience see what a speaker is talking about. However, the speaker should not assume that the audience will immediately understand what the image is and how it relates to the presentation. To speak effectively about visuals, guide your audience by doing the following:

• Tell your audience what they will see before you show the visual.
• Explain how the visual relates to your presentation.
• Point out two or three main features in the visual.
• Stand next to, but not in front of, your visual so that it is easy for your audience to see.

Speak effectively about visuals to guide your audience.

**Check your comprehension**

**A.** Watch a student give a presentation about the influence of geography on a place. Answer these two questions.

1. What city is the student talking about?

_____

2. What geographical features influence the city?

_____

_____

**Notice how the student speaks about visuals**

GO ONLINE

**B.** Watch the video again. Think about the information in the strategy box above. List two problems with the way the student speaks about the visual images.

_____

_____

_____

GO ONLINE

**C.** The student received some suggestions about his presentation and delivered it again. Watch the new presentation. List two improvements the student made to the way he spoke about the visual images.

_____

_____

_____

PRESENTATION
STRATEGY

**Strategies for Speaking Effectively about Visuals**

Prepare your audience for the visual image. Use language like the following:

- Here's a picture to show what I'm talking about.
- Let's look at a photograph. It will help you see what I mean.

Tell the audience what they are looking at. Point at the visual image. Use expressions like these:

- Here is . . . (name of something)
- If you look here, you see . . .
- To the right/left/north/south/east/west, . . .

**List more examples** **D.** Work with a partner to think of other ways to speak effectively about visuals. Write your examples here.

_____

_____

_____

**Practice speaking about visuals** **E.** Work in a group. Look at the four pictures on page 92. Have each student choose one of the pictures. Stand up in front of your group, and prepare the audience for the visual image. Tell the audience what they are looking at and how the geographical features in the picture might affect the culture of the area. Use the strategies for speaking effectively about visuals.

After you finish, have your classmates give you feedback. Ask them these two questions:

**1.** What are two ways I spoke effectively about the visual image?

**2.** What is one way to improve how I speak about visual images?

**Give a presentation** **F.** Develop and deliver a presentation about a place with an important geographical feature.

Choose a place that has an important geographical feature in or near it. Research how the place is influenced by the geographical feature.

Present what you learned to your class. Use at least one visual of the area. Use the strategies for speaking effectively about visuals.

Before you prepare your presentation, review the ideas and vocabulary from this chapter.

**A.** Work in a group. Research a sleep-related topic.

Go online, and research one of the following sleep disorders:

- hypersomnia
- restless legs syndrome
- insomnia
- sleep apnea
- narcolepsy
- sleep-walking

**Take Notes**
Take notes on the following information about the disorder:

- What are the symptoms?
- How many people does it affect?
- What treatments do doctors suggest?

**Discuss the Disorder**
Discuss the disorder in your group. Find out if anyone in the group knows someone with the disorder. Discuss how that person has dealt with the disorder. Share opinions about the best treatments.

**Present What You Learn**
Present a summary of the disorder, symptoms, and treatments. Organize your information into word visuals.

**B.** Work in a group. Study the local geographical features of your town.

**Take Notes**
Walk around your town or neighborhood, and take notes of:

- the geographical features you see.
- the geographical features' effect on the growth and development of the area (for example, how a river affects the flow of traffic).
- how people work with the geographical feature.

**Discuss the Results**
Discuss the results, and record them in a visual form.

**Present What You Learn**
Use your visuals to present your study to the class.

# Unit Goals

**UNIT**

**5**

# Humanities

**humanities** \hyuˈmænətiz\ The study of human constructs and concerns (such as philosophy, language, and the arts) rather than natural processes or social relations

**Think about the topic**

**A.** Look at the pictures of scenes from fairy tales. Then work with a partner to answer the questions below.

1. Which of the tales are you familiar with?

2. Describe what is happening in each picture. If you recognize the fairy tale, summarize the story.

3. Which fairy tales do you remember from your childhood? Why do you think you still remember the stories?

**B.** Read this information about the themes found in fairy tales.

## Common Themes in Fairy Tales

A child's world is rich with stories. The tales that children see in movies, read in books, or hear from parents take them on imaginary journeys. In these tales, children meet many strange and wonderful people, animals, or **creatures**. When we **take a step back**, however, it becomes clear that the stories are not quite as different from each other as they might first appear.

Fairy tales—these first stories told to children—contain many similar **themes**. These themes are also similar across cultures. No matter where a child is born, his or her fairy tales probably have **characters** like a poor servant girl who marries a prince, starving children who find a new home, or a young peasant boy who discovers that he is actually a lost king. In fact, the most popular theme in fairy tales involves a person's rising above his or her low position in life.

Another very common theme is caution. The main character, or **protagonist**, often receives a warning: "Be home before midnight," says the godmother to Cinderella. Fairy tales teach the young listener the terrible **consequences** of ignoring warnings. The message is predictable and clear: if you ignore the warning, you will suffer the consequences.

The **plots**, or story lines, of fairy tales vary, but they usually follow the same sort of progression:
1. The protagonist does not obey a warning or is unfairly treated.
2. He or she is sent away.
3. He or she must complete a difficult or dangerous task or must suffer in some other way to make everything right again.
4. He or she returns home in a better condition than before.

At some point in the fairy tale, the protagonist meets a mysterious person or creature. This person or creature helps by granting a wish or giving the character a special gift.

There is danger and drama, but most fairy tales end happily. The protagonist is successful and is rewarded with marriage, money, survival, and wisdom. And the **audience** learns an important lesson about life without ever leaving home.

**C.** With a partner, discuss these questions about the reading.

1. What is the definition of a fairy tale?

2. What are two of the most popular themes in fairy tales?

3. What is one of the lessons that children learn from fairy tales?

**D.** Match the words from the reading with their definitions. Look back at the reading on page 107 to check your answers.

____ **1.** creature     **a.** the people listening to or reading a story

____ **2.** theme     **b.** one of the players in a story

____ **3.** character     **c.** a living thing that is not a person

____ **4.** protagonist     **d.** the main message or lesson in a story

____ **5.** consequence     **e.** the events that form the main action of a story

____ **6.** plot     **f.** something that happens as a result of an action

____ **7.** audience     **g.** the main player in a story

**E.** Circle the phrase that best completes the meaning of the underlined idiom.

We know that fairy tales from different cultures have different characters and settings, but when we <u>take a step back,</u> we understand things _____ .

**a.** in a new way     **b.** in a better way     **c.** in the wrong way

**F.** Discuss these questions in a group. Share your answers with the class.

1. What are some of the lessons that you remember learning from fairy tales?

2. Name some of the characters that you remember from fairy tales. Why are they memorable?

**G.** With a partner, discuss three things that you have learned from the reading and from your discussion about fairy tales.

1. _____

2. _____

3. _____

**H.** To help you understand the listening strategy, discuss the situation below with a partner. Then answer the question.

During a lecture, the professor says, "Now, let me repeat that." What should you do?

**a.** Stop listening because you heard it already.

**b.** Listen carefully because the information must be important.

---

**LISTENING STRATEGY**

**Recognize Lecture Language That Signals When Information Is Important**

During a lecture, a professor will often communicate that he or she is making an important point and that you should pay special attention to it. When this happens, be sure to write the information down.

Listen for the words and expressions that professors use to signal an important piece of information.

**Expressions That Signal Important Information**

- This is important.
- It's important to note that . . .
- I want to point out . . .
- I'll say that again.
- Let me repeat that.
- You should write this down.

---

**I.** Work with a partner to think of other expressions that signal important information. Write your examples here.

_____

_____

---

**J.** Read these two parts of a lecture on the fairy tale "Cinderella." Then do the following:

- Circle the lecture language that signals an important piece of information.
- Underline the important piece of information.

Today we'll discuss a fairy tale that some say is the best-known fairy tale in the world. Take a minute and guess which one that is. . . . Did you guess "Cinderella"? If you did, you are correct. I want to point out that there are over 700 variations of the story. . . . Let me repeat that, . . . 700 variations of the story from many countries: Italy, Denmark, Vietnam, Russia, and France, to name a few.

Next class, we're having a quiz. I will include names and dates on the quiz, so it is important to write these in your notes now. One of the oldest versions of "Cinderella" is "Yeh-Shen" from China. The Chinese version of "Cinderella" dates back at least 1,000 years . . . from the 9th century.

**K.** Watch a short lecture about two characters. Match the first part of each sentence with the correct second part.

___ **1.** Cinderella has unkind      **a.** a different life.

___ **2.** Beth wants      **b.** family members.

___ **3.** Cinderella and Beth both want      **c.** a career.

Notice lecture
language for
important information

GO ONLINE

**L.** Watch the short lecture again. Write down the lecture language that signals an important piece of information. Then watch again, and write down the important information.

**1.** Important information lecture language: _____

_____

Important information: _____

_____

**2.** Important information lecture language: _____

_____

Important information: _____

_____

**3.** Important information lecture language: _____

_____

Important information: _____

_____

Learn general
academic words

**M.** Study the meaning of these general academic words. Fill in the blanks with the correct words in the correct form. Compare your answers with a partner.

**purpose:** the reason for doing or making something

**assume:** to think that something is true although there is no proof

People _____ many things about fairy tales without really thinking about them. Let's look at the _____ of fairy tales from an educational point of view.

**NOTE-TAKING STRATEGY**

**Highlight Important Ideas**

Professors let students know when an idea is especially important. When you listen to a lecture, highlight the important ideas in your notes by marking them in some way.

Read this excerpt from a lecture on fairy tales. Then look at one student's notes.

**Let's begin today by looking at the plot we find in a lot of fairy tales. It has five steps. Step one: the character is treated unkindly. Step one is the most common and important. Second, she receives help from a mysterious stranger. Then third, she meets a prince or someone else of a higher status in life. The fourth step: the character must prove her identity. Finally, . . . the fifth step . . . is marriage. Take "Cinderella," for example, . . . she marries the prince. He is the person of a higher status.**

**Here is a key question: Why do these stories usually have a character who is treated unkindly? What do you think? Well, this treatment is what helps the character look for change. Without the desire for change, there would be no tale. This is very important.**

| Plots in Fairy Tales |
| --- |
| 5 steps |
|     1. character treated unkindly *MOST COMMON +IMP * |
|     2. help from stranger |
|     3. meet person w/ more power |
|     4. prove identity |
|     5. marry person w/ more power |
| Why unkind treatment? |
|     helps character look for Δ *KEY* |

**Analyze the notes**

**A.** Use the excerpt and student notes above to answer these questions in your notebook.

1. How did the student highlight important ideas?

2. What were the two most important ideas in the lecture? How did the student show this in the notes?

**Highlight important ideas**

**B.** Read this excerpt from another lecture on fairy tales. Take notes, and highlight important ideas.

> I'd like to focus on one of the common themes that we see in fairy tales, . . . one idea that runs throughout every story—we must be cautious. . . . Let me repeat that idea, . . . we must live cautiously. In these tales, peace and happiness can only exist if warnings are obeyed. This idea is key to fairy tales.
>
> Let's look at a few examples. Cinderella can go to the ball, but she must be back when the clock strikes twelve. The king may invite fairies to the celebration for the new princess, but he must invite ALL the fairies, or terrible results will follow.
>
> This idea that we see in every story is very important, . . . the idea that all happiness depends on one action. All will be lost if one bad thing happens.

**Make predictions**
See page 8

**C.** Before the lecture, think about everything you have learned and discussed about fairy tales. What do you expect to learn from the lecture? Write three predictions below. Compare your predictions with a partner.

1. _____

2. _____

3. _____

**Watch the lecture**
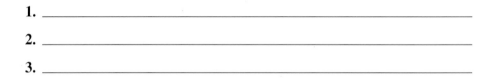

**D.** Watch the lecture, and take notes in your notebook. Highlight important ideas. Remember to listen for the lecture language that signals an important idea.

**E.** Circle the answer that best describes how well you were able to understand the lecture language.

I was able to recognize the signals for important ideas ___.

**a.** all of the time   **b.** most of the time   **c.** sometimes   **d.** not often

**F.** Use your notes to answer these questions.

1. What are some events in fairy tales that do not happen in ordinary life?

_____

_____

_____

2. Who were fairy tales written for?

_____

_____

3. What are the possible purposes of fairy tales?

_____

_____

_____

_____

4. Fairy tales are not just simple and childlike. How does the lecture describe them?

_____

_____

**G.** Were you able to answer the questions in Exercise F using the information in your notes? Compare and discuss your notes with a few other students. Help each other fill in any missing information. Revise your notes.

**H.** Work with a partner. Review your notes from the lecture. Then summarize the main points of the lecture for your partner. Take turns, and talk for 2–3 minutes only.

| ACADEMIC DISCUSSION STRATEGY | **Support Your Opinion** |
| --- | --- |

**Support Your Opinion**

Your opinions are more interesting and persuasive when you support them with details, examples, personal stories, and other information.

Use expressions to indicate that you are supporting your opinion.

**Expressions for Supporting Your Opinion**

I think . . .

- Let me tell you why.
- Let me give you an example.
- The reason is . . .
- This is because . . .

**List more examples**

**A.** Work with a partner to think of other expressons for supporting your opinion. Write your examples here.

_____

_____

_____

**Practice supporting your opinion**

**B.** In a group, read and discuss the questions. Keep the conversation going until every student has had a chance to practice supporting his or her opinions. Use your own ideas or the ones given below.

Many fairy tales have been made into movies: *Cinderella, Snow White, Beauty and the Beast, The Little Mermaid*, etc.

**1.** What are the advantages and disadvantages of seeing a movie version of a fairy tale?

**Possible Ideas**
beautiful scenery and costumes
Movies make it harder for children to use their imaginations.

**2.** What are the advantages and disadvantages of reading a fairy tale?

**Possible Ideas**
beautiful pictures
Written stories are sometimes scary to children.

**C.** **Discuss these ideas with your classmates. Remember to use the
expressions for supporting your opinion.**

1. The five most common fairy-tale plot elements can be summarized as
follows:

   • The protagonist lacks something.

   • The protagonist goes searching for what he or she lacks.

   • The protagonist meets a mysterious stranger.

   • The stranger helps the protagonist pass a test.

   • The protagonist receives a reward.

   Using these five themes, create a brief, original fairy tale. Try to use as
   many of the five themes as possible. Write notes below. Share your fairy
   tale with your classmates. After everyone shares his or her story, discuss
   how the tales were similar and different.

   _____

   _____

   _____

   _____

   _____

   _____

   _____

   _____

   _____

   _____

2. What other reasons might there be for people to read and enjoy fairy
   tales? Do film versions of fairy tales have the same purposes as
   written ones?

3. The lecture says that we may need fairy tales for wonder, entertainment,
   and education. What are some warnings that you received from fairy
   tales? What warnings do you think should be included in a modern fairy
   tale?

4. Look back at your notes. What was another idea in the lecture that
   you found important or interesting? Tell the class why you think it is
   important or interesting. Ask for your classmates' opinions.

**PRESENTATION STRATEGY**

### Emphasize Important Words

As you know, speakers use a variety of strategies—for example, body language, visual images, and rapport—to help their audiences follow their ideas. Speakers also emphasize important ideas in their presentations to help the audience understand which ideas are important. To emphasize a word means to pronounce the word with more stress—to say the word a little higher, longer, and louder. In general, emphasize words that are important to the topic and words that carry the most meaning in a sentence.

Emphasize important words to help the audience understand important information in your presentation.

---

**Notice emphasis of important words**

**A.** Read this short section of a group presentation of a fairy tale. The important words are underlined.

> Our fairy tale is called "The <u>Fountain of Youth</u>." . . . An <u>old</u> man and an <u>old</u> woman lived in the <u>mountains</u>. The man was a <u>woodcutter</u> . . . and the woman made <u>clothing</u>. One day, the man found a <u>spring</u> . . . —water coming from the ground . . . —and he <u>drank</u> the water. All of a sudden, he was <u>no longer</u> an old man. He changed into a <u>young</u> man. He was <u>so</u> happy . . . he <u>ran</u> home to tell his <u>old</u> wife. His wife said, "A <u>young</u> man should have a <u>young</u> wife." She said, "<u>I</u> will go drink from the spring, but <u>you</u> wait here." . . . He waited for <u>hours</u>, but she did not return. He went to find her, and when he got to the <u>spring</u>, . . . there was a <u>baby</u> by the spring. His wife had been <u>too eager</u>. She . . . drank <u>too</u> <u>much</u> water. The man was <u>sad</u>, and he carried his wife back home in his <u>arms</u>.

---

**Check your comprehension**

**B.** Watch a student give a presentation of this section of the story. Answer these two questions:

**1.** Who are the two people in the story?

_____

**2.** What happens to people who drink the water from the spring?

_____

---

**Notice emphasis of important words**

**C.** Watch the video again. Think about the information in the strategy box above. In your notebook, list two ways the student says the important words in the story.

_____

_____

GO ONLINE **D.** The student received some suggestions about his presentation and delivered it again. Watch the new presentation. In your notebook, list two improvements the student made to the way he emphasized certain words.

| PRESENTATION STRATEGY | **Strategies for Emphasizing Important Words**<br>• Say the word a little more loudly.<br>• Say the word with a slightly higher pitch. |
| --- | --- |

**List more examples**

**E.** Work with a partner to think of other ways to emphasize important words. Write your examples in your notebook.

**Practice emphasizing important words**

**F.** Stand in front of a group of classmates. Tell about one of your favorite fairy tales from your childhood. Give the title and a brief summary. To prepare, write down a summary of the story. Then underline the words that you want to emphasize.

Before you speak, tell your group four of the words that you want to emphasize. Practice the strategies for emphasizing important words.

After you finish, have your classmates give you feedback on how you emphasized important words. Ask them these two questions:

1. What are two ways I effectively emphasized important words?

2. What is one way to improve how I emphasize important words?

**Give a presentation**

**G.** Work with a partner to develop and deliver a presentation about a fairy tale.

First, choose a fairy tale from any culture in the world. Have one partner briefly tell the fairy tale in his or her own words. Have the other partner analyze the fairy tale. Explain which of the following plot elements are in the fairy tale:

• A character rises above his or her unfortunate position in life.

• A character receives a warning and suffers consequences for disobeying.

Use the strategies for emphasizing important words.

Before you prepare your presentation, review the ideas and vocabulary from this chapter.

**Think about the topic**   **A.** Look at the pictures of interesting buildings. Then work with a partner to answer the questions below.

1. Which photo most likely includes an office building? A restaurant? A hotel? A museum?

2. Do you like these buildings? Give reasons to support your opinion.

3. What are some interesting buildings where you live? What is interesting about them?

**B.** Read this online article about the form and function of buildings.

# DOES FORM FOLLOW FUNCTION? A SURPRISING STUDY

When you look at the outside of a building, can you tell whether it is an art museum, a library, or a theater? People often can't.

A recent study shows that many modern public buildings no longer follow the famous rule in **architecture: form** follows **function**. The idea behind this rule is that people should be able to understand the purpose of a building, or its function, from the way it looks, which is its form.

In the study, people in several countries were shown photographs of city halls, theaters, libraries, and art museums. The researchers asked the people to name the purpose of each building in the photographs. Surprisingly, people in the study chose correctly only 32 percent of the time. This shows that for many modern buildings, including the towering **skyscraper**, form does not follow function.

"The form of a building shows its meaning," said researcher Jack Nasar, who worked with Professor Kazunori Hanyu to conduct the study. "So it makes sense that **architects design** buildings to indicate their use. But our results suggest it doesn't often happen." In other words, people don't always know if the building is designed for **shelter**, for work, or for cultural activities.

The researchers in the study believe that when buildings clearly show their purpose, visitors can more easily find their way around the buildings, and city life is more comfortable and understandable for everyone. Some architects today are more interested in designing buildings to catch our attention than to tell people what goes on inside. Nasar and his team disagree with this idea: "You should be able to look at a building and have a good idea about what happens inside."

**C.** With a partner, discuss these questions about the reading.

1. What does *form follows function* mean?

2. What were the purpose and the result of the researchers' study?

3. Why do the researchers believe that form should follow function?

**D.** Circle the answer that correctly completes the definition of the underlined word. Look back at the reading on page 119 to check your answers.

1. Architecture is the style and design of a _____.

   **a.** machine          **b.** building

2. The form of a building is its _____.

   **a.** shape          **b.** purpose

3. The function of something is its _____.

   **a.** shape          **b.** purpose

4. A skyscraper is a very _____ modern building.

   **a.** ordinary          **b.** tall

5. An architect is a person who _____ a building.

   **a.** designs          **b.** researches

6. To design a building means to make _____ for a new building.

   **a.** an advertisement          **b.** a plan

7. Shelter usually refers to a place where people _____.

   **a.** live          **b.** work

**E.** Discuss these questions in a group. Share your answers with the class.

1. Is it important for architects to design buildings that indicate their use? Why or why not?

2. Look at the photos in the article on page 119. Why do you think the architects designed these buildings this way?

**F.** With a partner, discuss three things that you have learned from the reading and from your discussion about the form and function of buildings.

**Review the Listening Strategies**

Using the listening strategies in this book will help you better understand a lecture's organization and content. When you use these strategies, you will be able to recognize important information such as definitions, examples, explanations, and transitions to new ideas.

Review the strategies to be sure you can use them effectively.

**G.** Discuss the situation below, and think about all the listening strategies you have learned in this book.

Imagine that it is your first day of college. You sit down in a large lecture hall and get ready to listen to a two-hour lecture in English.

Which listening strategies could you use with confidence?

_____

Which listening strategies do you still need to practice?

_____

**Review listening strategies**

**H.** Write examples of lecture language for some of the strategies you feel less confident using. For help, look back at the listening strategies in this book.

**1.** Listening strategy: _____

Lecture language: _____

_____

**2.** Listening strategy: _____

Lecture language: _____

_____

**3.** Listening strategy: _____

Lecture language: _____

_____

**4.** Listening strategy: _____

Lecture language: _____

_____

**I.** Listen to a short lecture about architect Louis Sullivan. Match the first part of each sentence with the correct second part.

____ **1.** Sullivan believed that the skyscraper should celebrate

____ **2.** Sullivan believed that

____ **3.** Sullivan thought of

**a.** form follows function.

**b.** things ahead of anyone else.

**c.** its height.

**J.** Listen to the short lecture again. Write down examples of lecture language. Then listen again, and write down the information that follows the lecture language.

**1.** Topic lecture language: _____

Topic: _____

**2.** Big picture lecture language: _____

**3.** Transition lecture language: _____

New idea: _____

**4.** Definition lecture language: _____

Definition: _____

**5.** Example lecture language: _____

Example: _____

**6.** Explanation lecture language: _____

Explanation: _____

**7.** Important information lecture language: _____

Important information: _____

**K.** Study the meaning of these general academic words. Fill in the blanks with the correct words in the correct form. Compare your answers with a partner.

**point:** the most important idea that someone says about something

**concept:** the idea of something

The _____ I want to make is that the architect believed in the _____ that form should follow function.

**NOTE-TAKING STRATEGY**

### Review the Note-Taking Strategies

Using the note-taking strategies in this book will help you better recall the important information in your lectures when you study.

Review the note-taking strategies to be sure you can use them effectively.

Review note-taking strategies

**A.** Read this excerpt from the short lecture on architect Louis Sullivan. Then look at one student's notes. This student used six of the note-taking strategies you learned in this book. Identify the examples of note-taking strategies in the notes.

I'm going to cover some of the big ideas we got from Louis Sullivan because he's going to be very important to us in this class. . . .

Sullivan had many ideas about skyscrapers. And the thing you should know about Sullivan is that he was a true visionary. . . . By visionary, I mean someone who has the ability to imagine things for the future. . . .

So Sullivan had all these really new ideas . . . , for example, about the way to design skyscrapers. He believed that the skyscraper should celebrate and show off its height. So what I mean is, the skyscraper . . . should be tall and also be decorated with lots of attractive shapes. . . .

Sullivan is most famous for one particular idea. He said that, in architecture, form follows function. Let me repeat that: Form follows function. So the purpose of a building should help the architect create the design of the building.

---

Big ideas of Louis Sullivan

LS = visionary

    someone w/ great ability to imagine things for future

LS ideas

    skyscraper celebrates height

        should be tall + decorated w/ shapes

    * famous for FORM FOLLOWS FUNCTION

        (purpose indicates shape)

**Make predictions**

See page 8

**B.** Before the lecture, think about everything you have learned and discussed about architecture. What do you expect to learn from the lecture? Write three predictions below. Compare your predictions with a partner.

1. _____

2. _____

3. _____

**Watch the lecture**

**C.** Watch the lecture, and take notes in your notebook. Use as many of the note-taking strategies as you can. Remember to listen for all the lecture language that you have learned.

The Auditorium Building by Louis Sullivan and Dankmar Adler. Chicago, the U.S.

**D.** Check the statement that best describes how well you were able to understand lecture language.

_____ I was able to recognize most of the lecture language.

_____ I was able to recognize some of the lecture language.

**E.** Use your notes to answer these questions.

**1.** What was Louis Sullivan's famous idea?

_____

_____

**2.** What does Frank Gehry believe about form and function?

_____

_____

_____

_____

**3.** How does the professor describe the museum in Bilbao?

_____

_____

_____

_____

**4.** How well does the museum in Bilbao follow the idea that form follows function?

_____

_____

_____

**F.** Were you able to answer the questions in Exercise E using the information in your notes? Compare and discuss your notes with a few other students. Help each other fill in any missing information. Revise your notes.

**G.** Work with a partner. Review your notes from the lecture. Then summarize the main points of the lecture for your partner. Take turns, and talk for 2–3 minutes only.

**ACADEMIC DISCUSSION STRATEGY**

**Connect Your Ideas to Other Students' Ideas**

During a discussion, you may want to say something that is related to what another student said earlier. Be sure to acknowledge the other student's idea. This shows that you are paying attention, and it shows respect for the other person.

Use expressions to let everyone know that you want to connect your idea to another person's idea.

**Expressions for Connecting Your Ideas to Other Students' Ideas**
- My idea is similar to Anne's idea.
- As Anne already said/pointed out, . . .
- I'd like to go back to what Anne said.
- I'd like to go back to the point Anne made about . . .
- I agree/disagree with Anne that . . .
- Anne said. . . , and I'd like to add . . .

**List more examples**

**A.** Work with a partner to think of other expressions for connecting your ideas to someone else's ideas. Write your examples here.

_____

_____

_____

**Practice connecting ideas**

**B.** In a group, read and discuss the questions. Keep the conversation going until every student has had a chance to practice connecting his or her ideas to other students' ideas.

1. What are two or three of your favorite buildings? Why do you like them?

2. What do you think about skyscrapers? For example, would you like to work in one? Would you like to live in one? Why or why not?

**Discuss the ideas in the lecture**

**C.** Discuss these ideas with your classmates. Remember to use the expressions for connecting your ideas to others'.

1. Imagine that Louis Sullivan and Frank Gehry were asked to design a building together. What would it look like?

2. If you were an architect, would you be more like Louis Sullivan or Frank Gehry? Why?

3. Do you think people in the future will like Frank Gehry's buildings? Why or why not?

4. Look back at your notes. What was another idea in the lecture that you found important or interesting? Tell the class why you think it is important or interesting. Ask for your classmates' opinions.

The Cleveland Clinic Lou Ruvo Center for Brain Health by Frank Gehry. Las Vegas, the U.S.

**PRESENTATION STRATEGY**

### Pace Your Speech

When speakers are nervous, they often speak too fast. A fast pace makes it difficult for the audience to follow. To avoid speaking too fast, a speaker can make frequent, brief pauses throughout a presentation. Pauses help the audience listen carefully and understand the ideas. Therefore, it's important to know where and how often to pause.

As you speak, pace your speech. Group your words, and pause to help your audience follow.

**Check your comprehension**

**A.** Watch a student give a presentation about a famous architect. Answer these two questions.

   **1.** What is the name of the architect?

   _____

   **2.** Where are some of the architect's buildings?

   _____

**Notice the pacing**

**B.** Watch the video again. Think about the information in the strategy box above. In your notebook, list two problems with the way the student paces her speech.

**C.** The student received some suggestions about her presentation and delivered it again. Watch the new presentation while reading the transcript below. Mark with a slash (/) the places where the student pauses. In your notebook, list two improvements the student made to her pacing.

> Good afternoon, everybody. How many of you have seen this building? It was designed by an architect named Jacques Herzog. He is the famous architect I want to tell you about today. So let me give you some background on him.
>
> Jacques Herzog was born in 1950 in Switzerland, and that is the country where he works now. His architecture firm is in Switzerland, but he's designed buildings all around the world. For example, he's designed museums, stadiums, concert halls, and stores in America, Japan, China, and Spain.
>
> Now that I've told you about the architect's background, let me tell you about the interesting building I showed you that he designed that's in the United States.

**Strategies for Pacing Your Speech**
- Pause at the end of a phrase.
- Pause at the end of a clause.

**List more examples**

**D.** Work with a partner to think of other ways to pace your speech. Write your examples here.

_____

_____

**Practice pacing your speech**

**E.** Stand in front of a group of classmates. Tell the group about your dream house. A dream house is a house that you think is perfect in every way—its location, style, size, and design. You may want to draw a picture of your dream house first.

To prepare, write a description of your dream house. It should be about one paragraph long. Mark the places where you should pause. Practice the strategies for pacing your speech.

After you finish, have your classmates give you feedback on how you paced your speech. Ask them these two questions:

**1.** What are two ways I effectively paced my speech?

**2.** What is one way to improve how I pace my speech?

**Give a presentation**

**F.** Develop and deliver a presentation about a famous architect.

Choose an architect from the list below. Find information about the architect and his or her buildings.

| | | |
|---|---|---|
| Santiago Calatrava | Louis Kahn | Jorn Utzon |
| Elizabeth Diller | Rem Koolhaas | Paul Williams |
| Frank Gehry | Julia Morgan | Tom Wright |
| Zaha Hadid | Yoshi Taniguchi | |

Briefly tell about the architect. Include background information about the architect. Give examples of the architect's buildings and what makes them unique. Include pictures.

Use the strategies for pacing your speech.

Before you prepare your presentation, review the ideas and vocabulary from this chapter.

**A.** Work in a group. Choose a fairy tale that you and the people in your group are all familiar with.

### Discuss the Fairy Tale
Discuss the typical plot features of fairy tales that you learned about in Chapter 9. Use these features to analyze the theme, plot, and characters in the fairy tale you select.

### Take Notes
Write notes about how you might tell the same story with some surprising changes. For example, if you used the well-known Cinderella story, you could change it to include any of the following:

- Cinderella is ugly and has beautiful stepsisters.
- The prince can't dance.
- Instead of a slipper, Cinderella loses a cell phone.
- Instead of a carriage, she rides to the ball on a bicycle or a moped.

### Present the Tale
Tell your new version of the fairy tale to the class. Speak clearly, and pace your speech.

**B.** Work in a group. Create a survey of modern buildings.

Go online and find photographs of modern buildings. Then work with others to create a survey to test the form follows function rule.

### Listen and Take Notes
Listen to what people predict about the purpose of the buildings. Take notes of their answers.

### Discuss the Results
Work with your group to collect answers. How many people correctly guessed the buildings' purposes? Which buildings were the most surprising? Create a chart with your answers.

### Present Your Results
Present your survey and results to the class. Show the class your chart.

# ABOUT THE AUTHORS

### PEG SAROSY

Peg Sarosy is an Academic Coordinator at the American Language Institute at San Francisco State University. She previously taught at San Francisco State University in the ESL Program and the Design and Industry department. She also taught academic preparation at the University of California, Berkeley intensive English program and was a USIS Teacher Trainer in the Czech Republic. She has a Master's Degree in TESOL from San Francisco State University. Peg is co-author of *Lecture Ready 1* and *Lecture Ready 2*, and a series editor for *Lecture Ready 3*.

### KATHY SHERAK

Kathy Sherak is Director and Academic Coordinator at the American Language Institute at San Francisco State University. She previously taught in San Francisco State University's ESL Program and was a Fulbright Teacher Trainer in Italy. She is the author of the *Grammar Sense 3 Teacher's Book* from Oxford University Press. She has a Master's Degree in TESOL from San Francisco State University. Kathy is co-author of *Lecture Ready 1* and *Lecture Ready 2*, and a series editor for *Lecture Ready 3*.

# Notes